Praise for
Do You Hate the One You Love?

"With great skill and compassion, Joan E. Childs has written a thoughtful and insightful exploration of intimate relationships, complete with the struggles, conflicts, and disappointments that few of us can escape. She presents steps we can all take to build resilience and intimacy. Her message is clear, inspiring, and instructive. I encourage women everywhere to abandon their guilt and grab ahold of this book! If you've ever thought of leaving the man you love—the same one who can drive you to orgasm *and* anger in the same day—this book is essential reading."

—Susan G. Furman, psychologist, psychoanalyst, couples' therapist

"Leave it to Joan E. Childs to come up with a book title that could make most people say, 'Yes!' She displays a passionate attention to detail that matches her extensive training in the field, along with her keen interest and expertise in working with couples. She combines that with a charm and witty sense of humor, making her latest book an entertaining, compelling, and ultimately helpful read."

—Eileen J. Cohen, LMFT, MCAP

"In *Do You Hate the One You Love?*, a unisex and omnisexual journey to benefit us all, Joan Childs summarizes the many lessons and daily obstacles that derail couples, families, and individuals. Gleaned from her long personal and professional challenges, the book is academic and practical and will touch every reader who will recognize and find aid for familiar situations."

—Avram M. Cooperman, MD, FACS

"If you are looking for an informative, comprehensive, and practical book about the essentials of a conscious relationship, look no further. In *Do You Hate the One You Love?*, Joan E. Childs delves deep into the soul of our human connections. She eloquently illuminates the complex paradoxes of love, as well as the multigenerational secrets of Re-Pair, restoring our pairship. Weaving together psychological insight, science, practical examples, and storytelling, Joan richly gifts us with 'new eyes' to successfully navigate our journeys toward relational maturity."

—Hedy Schleifer, master relationship builder, founder of EcT (Encounter-centered Transformation), and author of *The Diary of an Amazon: Joining the Clan of the One-Breasted Women*

"With sensitivity and skill, Joan E. Childs gets right to the heart of the stumbling blocks all couples inevitably encounter in long-term relationships. The title of the book says it all. Sometimes we really do hate the one we love! Through fascinating case studies and exercises, Childs provides the tools we need to repair and renew our union."

—Christine Belleris, senior editor at Health Communications, Inc.

"Joan E. Childs is a generous friend, a trusted colleague, and an admired mentor. She continues to bless us with her wisdom and experience. In her latest book, Joan captures the essence of what it means to be female and our struggles to understand complex love and our attachment to men. Through theoretical and case studies, Joan leads us on a fascinating journey that is pragmatic and mystical. She's a great writer, and this is a book worth reading and saving on your bookshelf."

—Mary Kay Cocharo, LMFT, certified imago relationship therapist and practitioner of encounter-centered couples therapy

"This book provides an enthralling journey that explains how childhood trauma can lead us to 'hire and fire' our spouses (life partners) as we work through our issues. Childs uses vibrant, raw stories to depict levels of commitment we are capable of giving our partners, along with coping tools we can use to 'clean the environment' and create a sacred, safe space. This book has explained the conflicts in my relationships and given me tools to avoid communication gaps in the future. Thank you, Joan, for making the second half of my life easier to navigate!"

—Anne Melby, RMT, PMP, senior operations executive

"A refreshingly important read, written from the vantage point of a seasoned psychotherapist who has firsthand experience as a multi-divorced single parent with five children. In relating the stories of several female clients, Childs examines—with candor and wit—the conflicts and resolutions of each participant while offering professional wisdom."

—David Tabatsky, coauthor of *The Intelligent Divorce*

"Joan E. Childs illuminates each page of her new book with insightful examinations of our human connections. Some are strong, productive relationships, while others remain stuck in the depths of despair. In every case, we have much to learn from this talented teacher."

> —Richard Cravatts, PhD, President Emeritus of Scholars for Peace in the Middle East and author of *Dispatches from the Campus War Against Israel & Jews* and *Genocidal Liberalism: The University's Jihad Against Israel & Jews*

"Joan E. Childs examines the microscopy of interpersonal angst with full-blown, highly palpable clinical vignettes, which pique our interest from the outset. Her title captures the crucial theme and central tasks of most relationships. Her book reflects what often happens behind the closed doors of a psychotherapist's office. Her powerful examples of dysfunctional relationships and the various methodologies she uses to break down barriers to true intimacy demonstrate how she enables the development of healthy, durable relationships."

> —Jack Baruch, MD, diplomat of the American Board of Psychiatry and Neurology

"*Do You Hate the One You Love?* captures the true nature of the challenges we face in contemporary relationships. Joan's foundational knowledge of the best theorists and practitioners in the field is a perfect complement to her forty-plus years of professional experience. The technique exemplified in chapter 7 is spot-on for healing the wounds of our love relationships in a culture full of communication/connection chasms. Whether you're in a struggling relationship and longing for more love and connection or a clinician fine-tuning your expertise, this book is both invaluable and essential. Read away and watch the relationship transformation manifest!"

—Lisa Kelly Cargerman, PhD, MFT, Boulder, Colorado

"Written in an engaging, understandable style, *Do You Hate the One You Love?* allows the reader to be a fly on the wall at couples therapy as they uncover relationship conflicts, which often result from unconscious childhood traumas. Licensed clinical social worker Joan E. Childs shares her personal and clinical experiences to offer evidence-based approaches for those struggling in relationships, as well as for therapists working with clients addressing these issues. Equally skilled as a captivating presenter and an eloquent author, Joan's book is filled with the same wisdom and charisma she displays as a professional trainer, which she has done for MHASEFL's continuing education (CEU) programs. Satisfying relationships is a core element for maintaining good health, and this book provides the necessary strategies to achieve that goal."

—Marcia Pinck, Director at Florida Counseling Services Education & Outreach, Mental Health America of Southeast Florida

"I have known Joan Childs for more than thirty years as an outstanding therapist, and I am very familiar with her work. Not only has she been an inspiration to our family, but she has touched the hearts of hundreds of our students and faculty at Nova Southeastern University with her inspirational talks. She really cares about people, and her verbal statements are precious. She is indeed a 'rare bird.'"

—Stan Cohen, executive vice dean of the Health Professions Division, Nova Southeastern University

"Being exposed to Joan's lectures, I have benefited from the fountain of wisdom that she so generously shares. Life has taught her well, and she has been able to put the lessons to excellent use and share them in her unique way. She never ceases to amaze me. Her teachings can and have changed lives for the better. May she continue to bring her light to more places."

—Elahe Mehrel, EcCT

"Ladies and gentlemen, stop what you're doing, pick up this book, and buckle your seat belt. This book will blow your mind. It's a must-read! *Do You Hate the One You Love?* will touch the heart and soul of every human being. It addresses the core issues in all relationships. Joan writes like she talks—sassy and spontaneous, with wit, wisdom, and conviction. My hat is off to you, Ms. Childs. Thank you for putting all of this into an easy-to-read, well-written book."

—Adele Zum, Shoreside Connections, Inc.

"*Do You Hate the One You Love?* is a first-class primer on relationships! Peel back the layers of fears and desires. Joan Childs provides a psychotherapist's running commentary into two partners' struggles to be right. As each one gets vulnerable and relives his or her childhood traumas, they sympathize with each other, and new respect emerges. You will see yourself in these pages. If you are to create an authentic and intentional relationship, this is a must-read. Riveting!"

—Myles K Krieger MD

"I am a great fan of Joan Childs's work. She has long been a light in the field of recovering from childhood trauma, and I especially appreciate that she was an early proponent of John Bradshaw's work. I have referred many survivors to her, and I am delighted to hear that she has a new book on healing and saving relationships. I'm sure it will be packed with sage advice."

—Pete Walker, author of COMPLEX PTSD: From Surviving to Thriving and Holistically Treating Complex PTSD

"As an intuitive healer and relationship coach who guides individuals through the challenging processes of breaking up and rediscovering love, Joan's book profoundly expanded my understanding of the intricate dynamics of love-hate relationships. It provided invaluable tools and awareness to cultivate empathy and support my clients more effectively. Thank you, Joan, for opening my eyes to these crucial insights. I wholeheartedly recommend this book to anyone navigating the complexities of relationships, as well as to couples' therapists and coaches specializing in marriage counseling."

—Daniella Sol, intuitive healer and relationships coach and inspirational speaker

"*Do You Hate the One You Love?* by Joan E. Childs is a well-written and insightful guide, exploring the complexities of love and relationships. Joan does a phenomenal job showing how we can work together to solve challenges and conflicts in our partnerships. What sets this book apart is Joan's clever use of the word 'hate' in an unconventional way—not simply as a negative connotation but as a way to acknowledge the multifaceted nature of our partners. Through her wisdom, she teaches us that we must embrace our spouse in all their layers—the good, the bad, and even the ugly—to make relationships genuinely thrive. As someone approaching nineteen years of marriage, I trust Joan's expertise and the wisdom she brings to this book. As a published author, I wholeheartedly endorse this straightforward, easy-to-follow guide to navigating the ups and downs of love. Joan Childs is a true expert in her field, and this book is an invaluable resource for anyone looking to deepen their understanding of relationships."

    —Stacy Lee, author of the Prickly Pen Investigation Series & the Nubble Light Series

"Ladies, if your former Prince Charming now resembles the Prince of Darkness, you owe it to yourself and your relationship to buy this book. Filled with compelling stories of couples facing contemporary relationship issues, cutting-edge clinical research, and exercises to help couples grow stronger, this is a must-read for any woman who wonders, *Do I really want to spend the rest of my life with him?* or for any man yearning for a more soul-satisfying union."

    —Allison Janse, editor, Health Communications, Inc.

"I have known Joan Childs for more than thirty years as an outstanding therapist and a close family friend who has proved time and again her understanding of my family and our personal childhood traumas. Her book has inspired me to examine my own childhood trauma and learn how to work through personal issues with my children and my spouse. *Do You Hate the One You Love?* gave me the tools I needed to get through many stumbling blocks in my twenty-six-year relationship with my spouse. By practicing the tools given in her book, one is able to repair and mend one's relationship and even fall in love again. Joan Childs is a great writer, and this book is worth reading and rereading and to be given to those in long-term relationships."

—Hilit (Solomon) Sebag LCSW, CCCJS, MAC

"Childs's *Do You Hate the One You Love?* is a master class on relationships, packed into an easy read, chock-full of insights, examples, practical tools, and wisdom. It is a must-read for all women who seek to find harmony in their lives right now."

—Lori Pappas, entrepreneur, humanitarian, and author of *The Magic of Yes: Embrace the Wise Woman Within*

"Joan E. Childs, LCSW—psychotherapist, life coach, and inspirational speaker—has written this ultimate treatise on interpersonal relationships in the twenty-first century. Even though it is seemingly written by and for women, this particular guy (with a surgeon's type A personality) found it utterly engrossing and illuminative. A must-read for all—men included!"

—Stewart K. Lazow, MD, DDS, FACS (retired)

Do You Hate the One You Love?
Strategies for Healing and Saving Your Relationship

by Joan E. Childs

© Copyright 2025 Joan E. Childs

ISBN 979-8-88824-110-3

All rights reserved. No part of this publication may be reproduced, stored in a retrieval system, or transmitted in any form or by any means—electronic, mechanical, photocopy, recording, or any other—except for brief quotations in printed reviews, without the prior written permission of the author.

Designed by Suzanne Bradshaw.

Published by

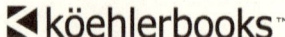

3705 Shore Drive
Virginia Beach, VA 23455
800-435-4811
www.koehlerbooks.com

Do You Hate the One You Love?

Strategies for Healing and Saving Your Relationship

Joan E. Childs

VIRGINIA BEACH
CAPE CHARLES

To Judith
and all the women and couples I have counseled.

Table of Contents

Foreword 1

Introduction: An Adventure in Intimacy 5

Chapter One: It's No Tempest in a Teapot:
It's a Big Deal! 17

Chapter Two: Why Can't a Man Be
More like a Woman? 30

Chapter Three: The Power of the Penis,
the Patriarchy, Politics, and the Pocketbook 40

Chapter Four: The Dangers, Drags, and Dubious Dregs
of the Dating Game 63

Chapter Five: Don't Fix It! Just Listen! 80

Chapter Six: No More Judgment, No More Criticism,
No More Blame, No More BS 97

Chapter Seven: Swimming to Paradise:
A Bridge Over Troubled Waters 115

Chapter Eight: Take Charge of Your Fears and
Reclaim Your Value 130

Chapter Nine: Where, Oh, Where Has
My Sexy Self Gone? 149

Chapter Ten: Coping with Post-Traumatic
Breakup Disorder (PTBD) 167

Chapter Eleven: A Conscious Relationship 183

Acknowledgments 195

References 197

About the Author 198

Foreword

I TELL MY STUDENTS that when my husband Yumi and I married in 1965, we were the Olympic champions of unconsciousness. Neither of us had any idea that there was such a thing as a conscious relationship.

Ernest Hemingway said, "The world breaks everyone and afterwards many are strong at the broken places."

Yumi and I began to explore how to become connected to each other from the "broken places" in our relationship. Expanding on what T.S. Eliot says about seeing a familiar place with new eyes, we arrived at a surprising discovery: our relationship is not a problem to be solved. It is an adventure to be lived and a gift to be unpacked. We discovered a guiding principle and three invisible connectors to productively live this adventure.

Here is the guiding principle. What will always disconnect us is the inevitable, reactive power struggle of our survival dance as a couple. What will always connect us is the mutual embrace of the three invisible connectors. The survival dance is our automatic reactivity to perceived danger in the relationship, which we import from our childhood narrative.

The three invisible connectors are the space, the bridge, and the encounter.

As a couple, we are responsible for the quality of the relational space. It is a sacred space and the playground of the children we bring to the world. We honor that relational space by crossing the bridge to the world of our partner to discover their culture and language. In doing so, we become bilingual and create together the conditions to experience the magic of what Martin Buber calls the encounter—a heart-to-heart and soul-to-soul connection.

I was fortunate to meet Joan Childs thirteen years ago at an important juncture in my own life. I had been married to Yumi for forty-one years and had just decided to create a master class for experienced couples therapists. I wanted to explore and share the relational paradigm and the encounter-centered couples transformation method, which had evolved from the living laboratory of my own marriage. To my delight, Joan, a seasoned psychotherapist and a person of experience and integrity, became an active participant in my master class, a three-year deep dive into the encounter-centered couples transformation method.

In *Do You Hate the One You Love?* Joan integrates her more than forty years of experience as a psychotherapist with 'new eyes' for the relational paradigm.

She says that "conflict is part of all relationships . . . a boundless, amorphous part of the human experience. . . . Content can be a friend when a couple cleans the relational space that too often becomes polluted over time. When a safe space becomes sacred and conscious, a couple moves their relationship forward."

We live in a time when we need to know more and more how to genuinely be close to one another. My friend, Lionel, says of the smartphone, "It's a device that decreases the distance between people who are far away and increases the distance between people who are close by." With our phones as indispensable as they have become in our daily lives, there is an urgent need for books about how to create conscious relationships.

This is the gift Joan offers. As you read, you will learn the skills to embrace and live the relational adventure. It is my greatest hope that you will come to enjoy the results that blossom in the living laboratory of your own relationships.

—Hedy Schleifer, master relationship builder
and author of *The Diary of an Amazon:
Joining the Clan of the One-Breasted Women*

Introduction

An Adventure in Intimacy

IN MY FORTY-SIX YEARS in private practice as a clinical social worker, more than 90 percent of my clients enter therapy due to a failing relationship, and nearly all of these "journeys" are initiated by women. This is not to say that men don't make the first call. It's just that they don't do it nearly as often as their female partners.

Men usually reach out after their wives or girlfriends have threatened to end the relationship or when they have been served with divorce papers. Women tend to contact me when they feel frustrated and disillusioned, hoping a seasoned therapist can restore their relationship. This process begins long before divorce becomes a consideration or an option. These women are hopeful that with the right counselor and a cooperative partner, things can get better, resolving conflict and healing their relationship.

Both parties are concerned about their children. What will happen to them if they are subjected to the fallout from a divorce? Men are especially fearful of losing access to their kids, and since their daily lives may already be overwhelming, this possibility may propel them into treatment. Somehow, men don't often hear the pleas from their partners as they share their pain and frustration. On many occasions, I have had to push men to attend couples' workshops and engage in therapy, while women are eager, often pleading to participate.

Do You Hate the One You Love? deals with the reasons men have such resistance to treatment, while women are anxious to resolve the issues and heal their bleeding hearts. In fact, while compiling a series of case studies, I conducted a test of several patients to gauge their interest in the subject of relationships. Women responded with enthusiasm, and the title piqued their interest. Many said they have felt that way more often than they cared to admit. The men I shared the title with responded without hesitation: "My wife would definitely read that book!"

To be clear, *Do You Hate the One You Love?* is not a male-bashing book. I love men, and as a therapist and hopeless romantic, I know many of them have experienced heartbreak, abuse, and a variety of "unmentionable" challenges in trying to make their relationships successful.

The title was born out of the mouths of some of my female clients—women caught up in a desperately messy mix of love and hate in their most important relationships. You might also be feeling simultaneously hopeful and hopeless. If that's the case, this book is for you!

Through specializing in couple's therapy, and as a multi-divorced single parent with five children, I have learned many things, but one fact is crystal clear: men usually reach out only after their wives or girlfriends have threatened to end the relationship or served divorce papers. At that point, it's often too late to repair what's been broken.

Women tend to reach out when they feel frustrated and disillusioned, hoping a therapist can restore their relationship. They hope that with the right counselor and a cooperative partner, things might improve by resolving conflicts and healing their relationship.

By making the first move—acknowledging a problem and

seeking help—they are on their way to finding a solution to this strange conundrum of hating the same person they love.

In all fairness, men experience similar issues, albeit less frequently, and when they do, they are not exactly willing to seek help. That's why this book could be the secret sauce they need. It might help some men become more aware and mindful that differences and conflicts with their partners can be negotiated when people decide to commit.

Aha! The C word. Commitment is at the root of many issues we see couples face today. When this is lacking for any reason, it illuminates the difficulties and frustrations women experience in their relationships with men, which is exemplified by the conflict we see repeating itself all the time: how oppositional feelings can simultaneously coexist.

For many couples, these challenges feel daunting, especially when the man or woman you married or live with becomes someone you despise as much as you adore. When that happens, and it usually takes time, what do you do? How do you handle your spouse or partner, and even more important, how do you take good care of yourself?

We can love our mate but also find their behavior intolerable. Does this sound familiar? Therapists refer to this condition as a love-hate relationship.

A 2017 study by Choosing Therapy.com reported that millennials attend couples therapy the most (51 percent), followed by baby boomers (48 percent), then Gen Xers (46 percent). In a study involving one thousand couples, approximately half said they attended some form of counseling with their spouse, and of those who had not tried any marital counseling, half were open to trying it. Are you? Is your partner?

In Tony Bennett's "Why Do People Fall in Love," he croons, "What do you call this condition when it hurts so good inside?" I'm sure you all know the feeling! This conundrum applies to how men and women feel about their partners, how parents sometimes feel about their children, and how children often regard their parents. It even affects us at work and in our communities.

As you read through the client stories in each chapter, revealing conflicts and resolutions, you will learn about rituals and exercises. In addition to anecdotal and empirical data, I also present peer-reviewed evidence cited by professionals and researchers, all of whom have explored relationships of all kinds, including Hedy Schleifer, internationally renowned master relationship builder, colleague, and author of *The Diary of an Amazon: Joining the Clan of the One-Breasted Women*.

Inspired by Hedy and many other peers and mentors, I have studied and examined why the emotional differences in men and women too often result in ineffective or damaging communication, which pollutes the relational space, resulting in a crisis.

In each chapter, I cite clinical encounters to introduce and analyze issues and conflicts. Solutions are offered to help couples avoid and resolve conflict and learn how to remain connected. I also highlight different aspects of how women experience conflict with their partners.

After all, conflict is part of all relationships, regardless of race, religion, creed, or culture. It is a boundless, amorphous part of the human experience. The content differs between each couple, but the structure and process of healing and repairing remain the same.

However, conflict can be a friend when a couple cleans the relational space that too often becomes polluted over time. When a safe space becomes sacred and conscious, a couple moves their relationship forward, often with the help and encouragement of a facilitating therapist.

Our collective mission is to understand the dynamics between the sexes and why more than 50 percent of marriages in the

United States fail (with subsequent marriages having an even higher percentage of failure). I have studied and examined why emotional differences in men and women frequently result in ineffective or damaging communication, polluting the intimate and trusting space any relationship needs, which ultimately leads to crisis. Having been exposed to the best and worst behavior, I often see that the core problems and real causes behind all these relationships in conflict can be traced back to childhood.

French novelist, critic, and essayist Marcel Proust said, "The real voyage of discovery consists not in seeking new landscapes, but in having new eyes."

That's exactly what I provide here!

This book began in my office while working with an estranged couple. Jackie's voice radiated from my office into the waiting room and hall. Her rage and hysteria sucked up all the oxygen in the room, leaving her husband and me in a state of shock.

"I hate him!"

She repeated this over and over.

"I hate this bastard, this dick, this asshole. He's a piece of shit!"

After she spelled out reasons to justify her feelings, she declared, "I'm done!" and rose from her chair, tossed a Prada bag over one shoulder, and slammed the door behind her as she fled my office. Her husband shrugged and said nothing.

Jackie returned a week later for an individual session and provided a laundry list of profanities to explain why she hated her husband. When I asked her why she remained in such a repulsive marriage, she looked at me wide-eyed as if the question almost made no sense.

"Because I love him."

"So, do you hate the man you love?"

"Yes, I do. When he's not acting like a dick, I find him lovable."

As I contemplated Jackie's statement, so full of passion and pain, I knew I almost had the title of my next book. I realized that similar words have filtered through my office endless times by women caught up in a love-hate relationship.

That night, I began to write, and nine months later, just like a pregnancy and birth, I completed my latest labor of love, which provided me with a sense of relief and a feeling of euphoria. Like any poet, artist, or musician operating in their zone of creativity, or a scientist, physician, or economist discovering their state of Zen, this process inevitably brings one's purpose into sharp focus. Once that laser beam shines bright, there is no turning it off until the "baby" is born.

Any new discovery cannot be automatically attributed to logic or reason. When we know we're onto something, the brain works in mysterious ways. The energy of the limbic and reptilian systems may need to dance with the neocortex, reminding us of our neuro-generative needs and to do things like eat, go to the bathroom, and walk the dog.

When I jumped into writing this book, I often walked my dog, Minnie, through the neighborhood, still in my pajamas, which is thankfully commonplace where I live. I was so excited to help Jackie and thousands of women like her. I know an audience is waiting for help to heal and repair their relationships. Many women and men need support and assistance.

Throughout the book, I highlight universal issues and values that emerge in every relationship, including health (physical and mental), politics, money, race, religion, sex, gender, and culture. They are all part of the human experience, and dealing with our differences is what matters. Only when we do can we communicate and heal.

Women will find aspects in each chapter showing how differently they experience conflict in their relationships, such as how they report and complain about their partners in individual and couple sessions. These challenges are ubiquitous, pervasive, and universal. Frustrations, which apply to gay and lesbian couples as well, include issues such as not being present, stonewalling, judging, ignoring, poor listening, and blaming.

We also include vignettes about women attracted to powerful men—celebrities, political figures, professional athletes, distinguished artists, and wealthy businessmen. These women pay a high price for their choices when they lose themselves to conquer their unconquerable guys. We see examples of this all the time, but these power struggles do not only exist on reality TV shows. They are rampant on all economic levels, where an unhealthy perversion of power by one party over another can poison a relationship.

One story about a woman held captive by her father to become his sex slave illustrates the power of the patriarch, which we cover in chapter two. Unfortunately, this story and many others are all too relevant in how they portray women's contemporary experiences. Just turn on CNN, Couples Therapy (Netflix), or one of many television shows to see reports of how unhealthy relationships are causing huge problems, both at home and throughout the world.

Just as I always aim to help couples solve conflicts and repair and restore their relationship, this book provides valuable resources to help you maintain a healthy and harmonious union. They include the valuable work of several marriage and family therapists, such as John Bradshaw, founding father of the self-help movement, who hosted numerous PBS programs focusing on codependency and spirituality, John Gottman, psychological researcher and clinician whose four decades of work on divorce prediction and marital stability led to The Gottman Method for developing lasting relationships, Esther Perel, a Belgian psychotherapist who promotes the concept of erotic intelligence in her book, *Mating in Captivity: Unlocking Erotic Intelligence*, Harville Hendrix, PhD, author of relationship self-help books, who, along with his wife, Helen LaKelly Hunt, PhD, is the creator of Imago Relationship Therapy, Lori and Morris Gordon, creators of the PAIRS (Practical Application of Intimate Relationship Skills) program, and, most recently, the work of Hedy Schleifer, a renowned marriage and family therapist who provides workshops all over the world.

The contributions of these highly respected experts have always informed my work and inspired the rituals and principles of a conscious relationship I am sharing here. While not every relationship can be healed, and some should end in a divorce or breakup, it's essential to remember that each partner must be totally committed to the reparation of a relationship to achieve a substantial and meaningful result. Just as a marriage is best when both parties are fully committed, so can a divorce be done best when both parties try their best to do it well.

We are all created with different parts, like a rainbow consisting of different colors. The total sum of our parts determines who we are and how we behave with others. You will learn how to negotiate these parts so that they can live harmoniously. This is what I do in my practice. Most folks are unaware of all their various parts, some of which are contradictory, and they struggle with internal conflict. This is normal. Consider the human body as a universe comprised of planets, stars, galaxies, and other forms of matter and energy. Just as the universe represents the total sum of its parts, we humans follow a similar pattern.

That means don't be alarmed! It's perfectly normal for oppositional feelings to coexist. It's common in parents with their children, and vice versa, employees with their employers, and in a plethora of family and communal relationships. Very little is black and white.

We are all perfectly imperfect. Just when you think you can't survive another minute with your man, your boss, your child, your mother-in-law, or your neighbor—let alone the rest of humanity—take a breath and calm down! This too shall pass.

I have learned that everyone is flawed to some degree. The challenge we face is how we deal with this reality, i.e., our flaws and those of our partner. What can you accept, and at what price? Your task is to be honest with yourself and your partner, which is easier said than done.

Do You Hate the One You Love? is an adventure in intimacy. Each chapter explores universal issues that crop up in any relationship and describes rituals and principles that can heal a contaminated space.

This book offers you a chance to investigate your relationships, define genuine love in your life, and make your relationship work. It's a bit like reading a book on swimming. The basic lesson is this: you've got to jump in the water before you can learn to swim.

That's the idea—jump right in. It's your turn.

I imagine the title of this book initially caught your attention because something about it resonates for you or someone you care about. That's the point: to help you heal and restore your relationships. I use the plural of that word for a reason. Of course, our primary focus is on the two people who constitute a marriage, but we all know that love-hate relationships can happen in any environment.

In today's world, the word "hate" carries all kinds of nasty connections and insidious meanings. It's aligned with hate crimes, societal divisiveness, mass shootings, political wars, anti-Semitism, Islamophobia, homophobia, and racism. Did I miss anything? Anyway, the point is, once social media and the press turn the word "hate" into a keyword for searches and monetizing the news, we're all in trouble.

But when push comes to shove, just as some of us form a love-hate relationship with our car, job, or hometown, we also often end up in love-hate relationships with our spouses or significant others. So, in a very real sense, we are always dealing with the yin-yang of love and hate, which I finally realized makes perfect sense to include in the title.

Google defines "hate" as to feel an intense or passionate dislike for (someone). Merriam-Webster's definition is an intense hostility and aversion, usually deriving from fear, anger, or sense of injury.

In the context of my book, "hate" merely defines the behavior of our mates, children, parents, friends, neighbors, and colleagues—not the person. We can have strong feelings of dislike when our children don't behave like we want. We can feel the same negative feelings when our spouse finds fault and judgment or when our parents punish us unfairly. We use the word "hate" to express simple anger, hurt, or feelings of disrespect and/or disenfranchisement. It's not necessarily loaded with the meaning and vitriol that we see in too much of today's vernacular.

During my time in private practice, many of my female clients have said, "I hate him. He's a jerk, unconscious, clueless, and doesn't know how to listen."

"So, why are you still with him?"

"Because I love him."

I would be rich if I had a dollar for every time . . .

As you can probably guess, it didn't take long for me to reply, "So, do you hate the one you love?"

A title was born.

These women explain that it's their man's behavior, not the man himself.

The conundrum is that I have never heard a man say, "I hate her." They may feel it, but they don't speak it out loud. Women seem to have the cornerstone of expressing hate for the man they love.

So, I use it as a title with my tongue firmly planted in my cheek, and I hope I have made this clear to anyone concerned with subsequent promotions, reviews, or sales.

For better or worse, "hate" has become an everyday part of our communication.

"I hate my job," or "I hate gefilte fish," or "I hate the man I love."

Any way you slice it, whether you're a mother whose kid "hates" carrots or you're someone who "hates" going a day without reading, it's just a word. As I often tell my patients, "Go ahead and hate him as long as you love him more."

When it comes to any challenging relationship, a sense of humor can go a long way, as demonstrated by the following two poems (both by anonymous authors). I think they provide the comic relief that men and women need when navigating the troubled waters of a marriage.

The Woman Poem
Before I lay me down to sleep, I pray for a man who's not a creep.
One who's handsome, smart, and strong.
One who loves to listen long.
One who thinks before he speaks.
One who'll call, not wait for weeks.
I pray he's rich and self-employed, and when I spend, won't be annoyed.
Will pull out my chair and hold my hand.
Massage my feet and help me stand.
Oh, send a king to make me queen.
A man who loves to cook and clean.
I pray this man will love no other.
And relish visits with my mother.

The Man Poem
I pray for a deaf-mute nymphomaniac gymnast
with big boobs who owns a bar on a golf course,

and loves to send me hunting, fishing, drinking, and motorcycling.
This doesn't rhyme but I don't give a shit.

Acquiring the basic skills for managing these dynamics will play a valuable role that will yield positive results beyond your primary relationship. This book uses many clinical encounters from my practice to introduce and analyze issues and conflicts. Whenever possible, solutions are offered to help you avoid and resolve conflict while learning how to remain connected.

Conflict is a part of all relationships and not something to run away from. It can become your friend, especially when a couple uses it to cleanse their relational space. When that shared space at home remains contaminated, it becomes hazardous, as each partner unwittingly reacts to a perceived or real danger occupying that shared space, affecting their life as a couple and a family. When that space is cleansed, it becomes sacred and conscious, and the couple (and their children) feel safe once again. As each party begins to relax, an actual change can occur in the brain and the central nervous system.

When this happens, the couple can move their relationship forward. This is the book's thesis—an adventure in intimacy with descriptive rituals and principles that heal the contaminated space.

In the words of Hedy Schleifer, whose TED talk, "The Power of Connection," has won rave reviews, "It is not a problem to be solved. It is an adventure to be embraced—a gift to be unpacked—a mystery to be understood and a secret to be uncovered."

Enjoy!

Chapter One

It's No Tempest in a Teapot: It's a Big Deal!

WHENEVER I WELCOME a new couple into my office for marriage counseling, I expect a few tense moments. After all, if everything was fine at home, they wouldn't be here. But when Jackie walked in with her husband a few years ago, I was not ready for the fireworks she brought.

"I hate that man!" she said. "I hate him! I hate him! I hate him! He's an asshole, a worthless piece of shit! He's a son of a bitch, motherf—er selfish bastard, and I hate him!"

Before I could get a word in, she rose to her feet, flinging her Prada bag over her shoulder, extending her neck stiffly while raising her chin to the ceiling in abject disgust.

"I'm done! &%$#@!"

Without waiting for my reaction or her husband's, Jackie stormed out of my office and slammed the door behind her. We could hear her continuing to curse, the sound of high heels reverberating in the hallway on her way to the elevator.

I forced a smile for Allen, who sat in silence, blushing with embarrassment. He shrugged his shoulders, threw up his hands, and apologized on behalf of his wife, seemingly clueless as to why she exploded in the first place. I had to wonder if this was accurate or if his blank canvas of a face was simply masking a much deeper problem.

How did we get here?

Jackie was not the first woman who ever fled my office, her knuckles white with blind rage as she grabbed her handbag. Although not every woman carries a Prada bag into my office, many bluster off in despair, carrying the burden of a troubled and anguished relationship. Jackie was not the first, and she won't be the last. However, on that day, when she exploded with such frustrated venom, the air in the room became so heavy so fast that it felt like a blast of carbon monoxide had permeated through my air conditioner. I felt an urgent need to walk into the hallway to escape the toxins Jackie had deposited on her way out. I excused myself for a few moments, as I had to take a few long breaths to restore my composure before I could return, sit calmly, and face Jackie's apparently clueless husband.

As I took my seat in what is ordinarily a lovely, comfortable chair, my mind was full of women's voices, in particular those deeply conflicted by their marriages. Before I could address Allen, who still appeared quite aloof and dumbfounded, I had to allow those voices their moment in my head before I could proceed.

"Sometimes I really hate him. I even despise him and wish I had never married him, but then there are times we have fun. We laugh together, enjoy a movie together, and just take a walk and hang out. But then as time goes on, we share less time with each other and argue more. The tension becomes palpable and throws me into despair when the space between us feels polluted and unsafe."

"It will never get better. Sometimes I think I'd be better off without him."

"I want to feel like I did the day we said our vows. I want to feel excited when he takes me in his arms, but those days are gone. We go to bed with our computers instead of each other, and we wake up each morning to the same displeasure we had the night before. Will we live in quiet desperation for the rest of our lives?"

"What's going to happen when our kids leave and it's just the two of us? How lonely will that be? What will happen if I get sick and he's not present or if he needs me in helpless moments in the years to come? Will my heart be in it, and will his be with me? What if I have a stroke or lose a breast, or what if he develops Alzheimer's or prostate cancer? How can we have each other's backs if we live in two different worlds, like doomed ships passing in the night?"

"I want my husband back! How did we drift so far apart? I don't remember when he seemed to disappear. Maybe it was when I disappeared in his eyes, after the baby was born, or when he got promoted and started working longer hours."

"Does he even remember the color of my eyes? I ache to return to the days when he told me he loved me. I'm sure he does, but he doesn't express it anymore."

"When my husband gets annoyed, he withdraws, and I'm left alone feeling abandoned and dismissed. How can we restore our love and reconnect?"

Fess up!

How often have you said these words under your breath (or even in an outburst)? How many times have you had these thoughts, wanting to throw something at your partner or husband, muttering or spewing a declaration of war or divorce?

Be honest! Don't feel guilty—it's a common response that occurs with chronic frustration when you don't feel heard, validated, acknowledged, valued, or respected—especially when nothing changes! Apologies are worthless when things stay the same.

You meet the love of your life, the man with whom you want to share your hopes and dreams. He's charming, warm, smart, handsome, sensitive, and loving. He can't get enough of you and you of him. But then one day you turn a corner, and out comes Mr. Hyde.

"Wait a minute! I didn't sign up for this. Where is Dr. Jekyll? Where is the man who swore to love and cherish me until death do us part? Who is this monster who came out of nowhere to torment me?"

Sound familiar?

He snores, he farts, he swears, and he never remembers to put down the toilet seat. The things you loved about him now piss you off. You don't remember this guy. He never listens, he talks over you, he lectures, and when you ask a question, he replies with a one-word answer—his favorite being "Yes" or what's become even more familiar, the instinctive "No."

"Is this the same guy I wanted to grow old with?"

"Do other women have these issues and feel alone and unloved in their relationship? Or am I the only one who has lost herself and her partner during all the time we've been together?"

Don't worry. You are not alone!

We're in This Together

These comments are typical of the diatribes I have continually heard from my female patients. Between the squeezed and painful tone of their complaints and the shrill sound of their frantic voices echoing their desperate sentiments, I often couldn't help but want to cover my ears and run out of my office. Is that because any of them are so terrible? No, not at all. It's because I can relate all too well as a woman and a wife. The truth is that I have felt and said many of these things myself, more times than I care to admit.

It's no surprise under circumstances like these that we are left to wonder why we get into these messes in the first place and why we respond so poorly when they don't work out the way we thought. That's because our brains are hardwired for making meaningful and trusting connections with people. When we experience a "disconnect," we go into crisis mode, as Jackie's reaction demonstrated. But of course, she is not the only woman in such a situation.

For example, Ellen—just thirty years old and a brand-new bride—had a meltdown less than thirty hours after her wedding. She and Mark had been living together for three years, and Ellen helped to subsidize the wedding and the townhouse they were living in, and she paid in advance for a honeymoon that never happened. She was unable to receive any support from her new husband or family in assisting and cooperating with the wedding plans. Instead, she was forced to go at it alone and quickly became exhausted from trying to make it all happen by herself. Where were the groom or his or her family members? I never had a chance to find out. Ellen was trying to make something work that was never destined to succeed. As soon as she realized that after the ceremony and the reception, she became overwhelmed, anxious, and exasperated by her husband's lack of care or concern. Her explosion in my office came because of her pent-up frustration and intense disappointment.

On top of that, Ellen suffered from depression, insomnia, anxiety, and intractable pain since she had contracted ankylosing spondylitis and fibromyalgia a few years earlier. These physical impairments, plus the emotional distress they created, had caused her to give up her job as an editor in a publishing company.

Once Ellen and Mark got home after the wedding, all hell broke loose. After she broke a vase expressing her rage, Mark called the police and requested that she be Baker-Acted. This is a Florida mental health act, enacted in 1971, which allows for involuntary examination (what some also call emergency or involuntary commitment), which judges, law enforcement officials, physicians, or mental health professionals can initiate for a period of up to seventy-two hours. There must be evidence that the person in question might have a mental illness.

To stop Mark from calling the police and starting that process, Ellen charged at him, trying to get the phone out of his hands. In the ensuing struggle, she accidentally knocked his glasses off, leaving him with a bloody laceration on his nose. This was the evidence he needed to prove that she was potentially harmful—to him and who knows who else—which would qualify her for admission to the psychiatric ward of a local hospital.

Although she was evaluated on the same day and discharged with no intention of harming anyone, including herself, Mark, the brand-new groom, decided right then and there that the short-lived marriage was over, and the next day, he went ahead and filed a petition for an annulment. He also locked Ellen out of their home, refused to return her belongings, and decided that she had been fraudulent with him by never revealing that she had issues with depression and anxiety, although, according to her, he had known this since before they even moved in together.

What's Really Going on Here?

I have to jump in here and say that I find it hard to believe that Mark had no idea that Ellen was suffering from numerous ailments. No matter how hard she may have tried to conceal her struggles, how could he not have known anything about them? Can we take a chance and call him clueless, or would that be presumptuous and a minor case of male-bashing? Since we don't want to be guilty of either charge, let's investigate further.

Under normal circumstances, Ellen would never have been considered a violent woman. With mitigating circumstances, however, surrounding the wedding, unable to properly attend to the details of her big day, coupled with dealing with intractable, chronic pain, with little or no support from her new husband, her inner beast rose from the coals of hell, blowing dragon fire from the depths of her being. All the turmoil, frustration, and lack of communication became fodder for a perfect storm! There was no taming this shrew.

"Hell hath no fury like a woman scorned!"

Shakespeare was right, and I'm sure he would have winked at me if he had been a fly on the wall that day in my office. He was not the only one. Countless writers, psychologists, and philosophers have opined on how women deal with the frustrations and angst they experience in their relationships. I have heard it from the source, from women, me included, who keep reminding me how different women are from men.

John Gray was spot-on with *Men Are from Mars, Women Are from Venus*, what has become the Bible for understanding the difference between us since it was published in 1992.

Meet Your Biology

Between all the therapy I have had and all the couples I have counseled, including Jackie and Alex and Ellen and Mark, Gray's words are endemic to living in any relationship between two sexes. I continually ask myself why these words and feelings are so unrelenting. After all the creative marriage and couple counseling techniques I have studied and practiced and the various modalities I have subjected myself to, how is it that these sentiments continue to persist? I have finally figured out the answer. It requires understanding a bit of biology, coupled with acknowledging some crappy role-modeling and early interventions inscribed into the brains of boys who eventually become men.

"You wanna cry? I'll give you something to cry about!"

"What are you, a sissy? Boys don't cry! That's for sissies or girls!"

"Be a man! Act like a man!"

"You're not scared! Boys are strong. We're tough! Only girls get scared! Get over it!"

"You got feelings? I'll give you a feeling right in your face!"

These examples may sound a bit dated, especially if you consider yourself a "progressive" parent, but they can also take shape in more subtle ways.

"Come on, you're such a big boy. Big boys don't cry."

"Just throw me the ball. Throw it like a boy!"

"Act like a man? What are you, a girl?"

"Don't tell me you're scared like your sister, are you?"

"It's fine to have feelings, but boys shouldn't talk about them too much."

Back in the day, and still now in many cultures and subcultures, anytime a boy has a feeling, it is linked with shame or embarrassment. Boys consequently learn early in life not to feel or show feelings. If a situation became too emotional, everyone would vacate the premises, except for perhaps Mom and any other concerned females. Any efforts by Mom to console her son were often interrupted with challenging comments, such as, "Don't baby him," or "Stop coddling him. He needs to toughen up!" As a result, boys grew up to become split off from any feelings of sadness or hurt. Anger became a more acceptable response.

"Somebody hit you? You hit them back!"

"Oh, Johnny hurt your feelings? Well, then, you go ahead and hurt his face!"

"Sticks and stones, boy, sticks and stones. Just shut up and play ball."

Anger is often a boy's first response to being hurt, which doesn't stop when he becomes a man. Since boys are conditioned to feel shame for showing hurt or weaknesses, they use anger as a means of reacting, often to no good outcome. Girls, meanwhile, are often shamed for anger.

"Don't be sassy with me!"

"Girls are supposed to be little ladies, so act like one."

"Just sit there quietly until you get over yourself!"

Instead of showing anger, girls cry, almost like a default mechanism. If men could express their fear and sadness without shame, and women could express their anger without shame, we would all live happily ever after! Sounds easy, but it's not.

Our Real Challenge

We now know that early imprints from society and parental attitudes at home form the foundation for our being. Neurobiologists have substantiated and documented empirical evidence that our minds, personalities, and behaviors are influenced more by our environment than our genes. It's true that genes give us a predisposition to who we become, but lifestyle, environmental factors, and culture trump genes!

In *The Biology of Belief,* Bruce Lipton, PhD, an iconic cell biologist, draws evidence from studies in cellular biology that support his theory. The good news is that we can change, but only if we choose to and learn the appropriate ropes.

Hard to imagine? It's true. The results play out in our most important relationships—those we choose to be our life partners. This is not a blame game. If we had to blame our parents for poor parenting, we would have to go back to their parents, the parents before them, and so on. That would become futile and leave us taking no responsibility for who we are and how we behave. It also means we would shirk what should be a welcome responsibility as role models.

Our challenge and obligation is to know what the hell happened to us and act so we become conscious of our behaviors. We must be conscious of our behavior and take responsibility for it!

Change is not only possible. It is necessary to enjoy a life of joy and fulfillment. We can choose to make the necessary changes to live our lives in the sacred space we longed for when we took vows.

As young brides and grooms, we know little about how our past influences our present. As adults and parents, we must move our relationships forward and make our relational space safe for each other and our children, learning why we do what we do and its effect on our life partner.

The Truth Always Surfaces

I have been fortunate to study psychology with the best of the best. I was trained in PAIRS with Lori and Morris Gordon, certified with John Bradshaw in Creating Healthy Relationships, and attended workshops, seminars, and lectures with Harville Hendrix, PhD, author of *Getting the Love You Want* and founder of Imago Relationship Therapy. I've studied the works of John Gottman, an American psychological researcher and clinician who has done extensive work on divorce prediction and marital stability, and Sue Johnson, a psychologist specializing in bonding, attachment, and adult romantic relationships and who, along with Dr. Leslie Greenberg, developed Emotionally Focused Therapy (EFT) and founded the International Centre for Excellence in Emotionally Focused Therapy (ICEEFT), a therapist training institute. I have also researched Esther Perel, therapist, author, and creator of the groundbreaking podcast *Where Should We Begin*, and most recently, at the age of seventy-five, I took a three-year master class called Encounter-Centered Couples Therapy with a wonderful group of masters in their various therapeutic disciplines who brought great ideas, skills, and methodologies to couple counseling, all led by Hedy Schleifer, whose TED talk, "The Power of Connection," describes the Three Invisible Connectors: the Relational Space, the Bridge, and the Encounter.

In many cases, the results were miraculous, transformational, and enduring. But eventually, after many two-day intensives and three-day workshops, the "I hate him!" energy would resurface and show its nasty ass once again. Couples who engaged in couple's therapy were at least aware of the cause—even the implications and consequences—but were still unable to contain the feelings that were triggered in a split second.

When one partner felt triggered by a word, a look, silence, a judgment, or dismissal, they acted out what came naturally, and that, we must all admit, is not always healthy. The shouting resumed, the tears and hysterics recycled, doors slammed, and the space that was once sacred became polluted and messy once again. Not surprisingly, the other partner usually became reactive or withdrew into what I call a silent violence.

What Do We Do Now?

When each person in a relationship falls into survival mode, as if it's a default mechanism, the tension will always mount. It's a simple guarantee of biology and psychology, mixed in a volatile combination. A person's essence gets lost in the muck and mire of conflict, and they operate out of survival patterns they unwittingly learned in childhood. In her workshop, An Adventure in Intimacy, Hedy Schleifer explains that couples unconsciously choose the perfect person to bring them the biggest nightmare to help resolve early childhood traumas. They unwittingly hire their partners only to fire them for doing the exact job they had hired them to do. What a conundrum!

This is an issue that has plagued men and women throughout the ages. It has been studied, researched, and written about by scientists, biologists, social psychologists, psychologists, psychiatrists, neurobiologists, philosophers, mental health providers, marriage and family counselors, sex therapists, social workers, clergy, and even lay people.

Notice how I've referred to both men and women being affected by these endless cycles. This is not about male-bashing or laying blame anywhere—other than with all of us. That's because we are all responsible for our choices—good, bad, or somewhere in between.

Let's move on with the mystery of biology and social conditioning, which stimulates all women to figure out why men behave the way they do instead of acting more like us.

Heav'n has no rage,
like love to hatred turn'd
Nor Hell a fury,
like a woman scorn'd.

—WILLIAM CONGREVE (THE MOURNING BRIDE)

Chapter Two

Why Can't a Man Be More Like a Woman?

IN THE LEGENDARY 1964 Broadway musical *My Fair Lady*, lamenting the state of affairs between men and women, appears a rhetorical question: "Why can't a woman be more like a man?"

I prefer to take the opposite approach: Why can't a man be more like a woman?

Although song and dance is not my specialty, if I could chant this phrase with the same wonder and curiosity that Rex Harrison possessed in his role as Henry Higgins, I would definitely do so, albeit without the clever British accent.

"Why can't a woman be more like a man?"

Because she doesn't want to be! Period.

Why can't a man be more like a woman?

Essentially, because they're not!

We know this from biology, anthropology, and social conditioning, and on paper, it appears so damn simple, so why all the emotional fuss and perpetual problems? When Henry Higgins appears to be tortured by the whimsical Eliza, it's because she is a woman who wants to be herself. He becomes obsessed with turning her into what he thinks she ought to be according to his standards and expectations of femininity. As suspected, Eliza subjugates her will to his and becomes the elegant, fashionable Miss Doolittle he created as his fantasy woman.

The Stigma of Role-Playing

I emphasize the word fantasy, as this is largely what it was back then, and it still is. While Higgins takes the role of a Svengali in elevating Eliza from an impoverished flower peddler to the belle of the ball, it reeks of superficiality and seems quite unsatisfying in today's evolved climate. As much as Rex Harrison made Henry Higgins seem charming, what price did Eliza Doolittle actually pay? I mean, what happened to the authentic Eliza?

To please him, she loses her essence. When she realizes she has been used for his aspirations, she becomes enraged and enjoys a genuine fit of violence. She heaves his slippers and lunges at him, beating him with a vengeance so unlike the Miss Doolittle he once created. Her rage is finally unleashed, and he has no clue why.

Hmm, sound familiar?

We might be relieved that it was just a play (and movie), and we can accept the literary license to tell a story, but at what cost? What roles did this story perpetuate? In truth, Eliza was not so different from Jackie, the woman who stormed out of my office in a fit of rage while her husband looked on in dismay. Both were victims of society placing a stigma on their choice to be independent women, regardless of an unsupportive environment.

Repeating the Past

Popular songs like Tammy Wynette's "Stand By Your Man" and "Master of the House," from the Broadway musical, *Les Misérables*, portray men in opposite ways as they reinforce gender stereotypes and describe how many women feel about their men–for better or for worse.

While catchy lyrics that honor men or let them have it may

inspire us when they're recited by a singer we like, many women in crisis will find those same words and ideas troublesome, especially when they reveal deep problems in their real life.

How many women do you know who are living out the fantasy of what their male partners expect and demand? How many are in pain from not feeling accepted as they are? How many are living in quiet desperation or have become shrews in a marriage that emulates what happens in Edward Albee's play, *Who's Afraid of Virginia Woolf?* How many women are currently surviving and perhaps even enjoying a sadomasochistic relationship?

Despite whatever progress the women's movement has made, these questions remain sadly relevant in today's world. Many women continue putting up with behaviors from their mates that any psychotherapist would call abusive, tormenting, disparaging, insulting, disrespectful, inconsiderate, and unacceptable.

Is it out of fear of never finding someone better?

Is it because of economic insecurity?

Is it that women stay put to protect their children from the risk of separation?

Perhaps the submission and capitulation we often see is due to the supposed theory that the grass is never greener on the other side. Perhaps it originates with what these women know from having grown up in their families of origin.

Whatever the reason or rationale might be, women are guilty many times over of losing their essence for the sake of having and keeping a man.

A Deal with the Devil

The scary part is that many of them are not even aware of the trade-offs they have made, such as security in exchange for authenticity, compliance in exchange for legitimacy, not rocking the boat in exchange for peace, and losing their voice in exchange for their essence.

Are any of these just a recapitulation of their past? Are women who do these things reverting to choices that were once so familiar that they now feel normal or natural?

Either way and for whatever reason, they are making a deal with the devil.

Sigmund Freud called this type of behavior repetition compulsion, which he described as the need to repeat the past. Alice Miller, psychiatrist and author of *The Drama of the Gifted Child*, called it "the art of absurdity."

We only know what we know! Our brains are wired to perpetuate what is familiar. The past creeps into the present without warning or conscious awareness. Suddenly, almost out of the blue, we find ourselves married to our father or mother, depending on which parent caused the most conflict and damage or who we most identified with as a child.

To run from the past, we drag it into the present, finding a replacement for the person we are running from. In essence, we are addicted to our past, and the only way we can break away from it is to understand the cause, but not just intellectually. It must be relived with a trained professional in an experiential therapeutic setting. Instead, people opt for drugs as their preferred treatment, which usually only mask the symptoms instead of dealing with them effectively. Drugs, whether prescribed or illegal, are not the ultimate panacea. When dealing with the devil, genuine resolution takes process, time, money, and commitment, which may be too much for the average person. Divorce, which can be costly, is often chosen as an optimal solution.

"We just weren't a good match."

"I've had enough."

"It was inevitable."

These are just a sample of typical explanations.

The Love-Hate Conundrum

How can I hate someone I love? Any woman reading this already knows the answer. It doesn't take an expert to know that "the dude" is not monolithic. He has a variety of parts, like we all do. He can be loving, generous, considerate, sweet, understanding, supportive, and smart. He can also be intimidating, judgmental, unemotional, contemptuous, stonewalling, and critical.

The most difficult behavior for a man is to be present and communicative as he tries to see your world through *your* eyes and ears, recognizing that you are carrying your past just as he is carrying his.

Each of you is depositing your past into the relational space we call "the relationship." After years of dysfunctional behavior, that space can become polluted, and neither of you knows how to fix it. When that happens, love flies out the window as the language of disillusion and frustration wields its nasty head. That's when the "I hate him" refrain reverberates through the windows of your mind and sometimes your mouth!

Remorse for lowering your standard of acceptable behavior follows. The guilt and shame after speaking harsh words are worse than the feelings that caused the initial clash.

However, the damage may already be done; the words can never be retrieved. Only apologies offer hope for forgiveness. In cases like this, all is well until it's not. As day follows night and night follows day, the pattern returns. It may reappear with different content but the same results. The pollution mounts, the space is no longer safe, and the mutterings and spewing return.

This polluted space becomes a toxic playground for your children and pets. Innocent animals know how to escape and hide under a bed. Children, not so much. Even worse, many children—of all ages—feel responsible for the cause of their parent's strife and guilty for not being able to fix it. These feelings of helplessness become the foundation of their survival self. As they grow into adulthood, they seek partners who unwittingly play out their dysfunctional past. This cycle becomes their present by recreating multigenerational toxic shame.

It's a heavy load for any child, adolescent, or young adult to carry.

Same Species, Different Brain

During his comical and highly entertaining video, *Tale of Two Brains*, marriage expert, minister, and author Mark Gungor illustrates how a man's brain differs from a woman's. He places two brains on two podiums, one representing a man and the other a woman. His presentation to the audience is not only hilarious; it's chock-full of fascinating content.

He claims that men have an empty box in their brains that, if provided with the desired content, would be filled with empathy and heartfelt emotions. On the other hand, women have a box in their brains already filled to capacity with empathy and emotions.

When a woman tries to engage her male counterpart with these parts, the ones that come naturally with being a woman, the man, who is void of these inherent parts, can't automatically relate to or understand her needs and desires. They simply do not compute.

A simple solution—one of many, I'm sure, most any woman may conjure—probably seems like an impossible mission. But she will try to "convert" him, as if she thinks she is the one and only woman in the world who can. That's also in her DNA. But it doesn't work, just like it won't work when a woman thinks she can convert a gay man to be straight.

As a result, the battle of the sexes persists. A woman will remain frustrated until somebody can fill up the empty box of her man with the missing ingredients that do not automatically appear inside his brain. Some women can be patient with this and maintain reasonable expectations for their partner. Other women keep the bar raised too high and end up disappointed. That's like expecting a man without legs to suddenly get up and walk or a cat to bark when someone is at the door. A miracle might create a new outcome, but since when are women, as amazing as we admittedly are, expected to be miracle workers?

Pets Have Feelings, Too

I have two dogs, Minnie, a thirteen-pound Shih Tzu, and Motik, a thirteen-pound Pekingese. Motik is short for Motik Shallee, which means "My Sweetie" in Hebrew. When we go for our walks, Minnie, a female, pees once. Motik, a male, seems compelled to pee on every blade of self-selected grass, every tree, every fire hydrant, every fallen leaf, every tire, and every rolled-up newspaper. He marks his territory at least fifteen times compared to the elegance of Minnie's one release. Motik shuffles, kicks, and gyrates from side to side as if in a Zumba class. Our neighbors call him Fred Astaire. He just can't help it. He's a guy and can't help lifting his leg at least fifteen times. It's in his nature, an essential part of his DNA. Minnie, whom I've nicknamed Ginger Rogers, patiently waits for him or ignores what he's doing. I have to wait for him to squirt as often as he likes until he feels satisfied. It's not rocket science. It's a male dog who needs to pee. For some reason, it makes him feel good, so what's the harm besides some wet grass, a few damp leaves, and a soggy headline or two?

If women could accept the difference in gender as I do with my dogs, relationships would be so much easier. There would be no disappointment, disillusionment, or bitterness. We seem to accept canine behavior more easily than human behavior! Maybe if you remember that your man is also your pet, this philosophy will become more useful.

Just sayin'...

To assume that men don't have feelings is an erroneous

assumption. They have decidedly strong feelings, including fears that they are out of touch with or too frightened to admit how they feel, as it might make them seem like less of a man.

Men have needs exactly like women. There, I said it. They want to feel loved and respected. They want to matter, just like women. Unfortunately, they have not learned the art of expressing themselves because they were shamed or not taken seriously when they tried it as children or young adults.

This lack of communication creates a barrier in any relationship. She can't read his mind, and he can't read hers. They unconsciously fear the same response they received as a child but don't know it consciously, so instead, they stay silent or act it out, often through anger. When this happens, the chasm grows wider. However, if both parties take the time to learn each other's feelings and needs, their responses will change.

The bitch he calls his wife or partner can morph into a gentle, appreciative, and loving woman. The husband, a.k.a. the asshole, can become engaging, empathic, supportive, and understanding. It's a movable and flexible dynamic!

Consider this: does a husband drink because his wife nags him all the time, or does a wife nag because her husband drinks too much?

It doesn't matter. Someone has to make a change. Either he stops drinking, or she stops nagging. When this occurs, when they keep their eye on the prize and behave without unbearable tension and strife, their dynamic will change.

What Do We Do Now?

Philosopher Martin Buber maintained that humans are hardwired for meaningful connections and that when we disconnect from each other, we enter into a crisis. The only way to overcome this is to learn how to reconnect. First, we must be willing, and then we have to agree to make the effort. You will find much more on learning how to reconnect in chapter ten.

You may still be wondering why a man can't be more like a woman. Face it. They can't, unless they choose to stretch their emotional muscles and maximize their growth potential without feeling threatened that they will compromise or lose their masculinity, pride, or ego. This might be a big ask for some and a real reach for others, but being open to perpetual possibilities and personal growth doesn't make a man any less of a man. In fact, it will make him more of a man as he becomes even more humane!

As for you women, dream big and be patient.

One's dignity may be assaulted, vandalized and cruelly mocked, but it can never be taken away unless it is surrendered.

—MICHAEL J. FOX

Chapter Three

The Power of the Penis, the Patriarchy, Politics, and the Pocketbook

WHEN SHAKESPEARE WROTE, "Something is rotten in the state of Denmark," he could have easily expanded the list to include our entire nation. Since the days of the Neanderthals, men in power have felt they have the right to abuse people, and in particular, they feel entitled to commit sexual misconduct. Whether it's Roy Moore, Harvey Weinstein, Bill Cosby, Charlie Rose, Al Franken, Anthony Weiner, Donald Trump, or other high-profile celebrities or politicians, occupying a powerful position does not give any of them the right to assault, batter, harass, grope, or objectify women—at home, in the workplace, or anywhere else.

Predators have many faces, and they are not all politicians, movie stars, or athletes. They are doctors, lawyers, judges, businessmen, and professors, and most of them are also husbands, boyfriends, fathers, grandfathers, uncles, cousins, sons, or neighbors. Any man, young or old, rich or poor, or Black or White, who feels that he has the right to take advantage of a child or woman without consent is a predator.

End of story.

With the explosion of social media, more men cannot get

away with their behavior. We used to have no way to record the abominable habits of powerful men, but we live in a different age, which means the crimes and transgressions of bad men can be revealed for the world to see. And women are finally standing up and raising their voices to say, "Enough is enough!"

Our new heroines can be found in the halls of Congress, boardrooms on Wall Street, and courtrooms throughout the country. Kudos to those ladies for doing the right thing. They empower other women to stand up to their perpetrators and courageously share their stories.

How Does This Begin?

Early in life, usually long before we know who we are, we fall in love, lose our minds, and commit to men we may not even know very well. As we gaze into each other's eyes, our boundaries collapse, and we think we have made a connection that will last forever. We are young, in love with love, and full of magical thinking, hopes, and dreams that we will live happily ever after—with this one special man.

"Till death do us part," we say in our wedding vows, unaware of how deeply we've been affected by our culture and the mythology of love. Ever since childhood, we've been inundated with songs of romantic love, heartbreak, codependency, and loss, all of which support our myths.

"I can't live if living is without you."

"It cost me a lot, but there's one thing that I've got, and it's my man."

"For whatever my man is, I am his forever more."

We have our favorites, whether they have come to fruition or not.

Romantic movies usually feature happy endings, such as Sleepless in Seattle, Love Actually, and many more. Children grow up on Disney movies, which portray classic formulas we can only dream of: girl meets boy, boy meets girl, boy rescues girl, or girl falls in love with her heroic knight in shining armor, and they live happily ever after. Girls grow into women, however, forever searching . . .

News flash: the only knights available are wearing rusty armor.

We grow up believing in the fairy tales and stuff of dreams that have been projected on a screen or heard in music. We know it just ain't so, but something keeps us trying to make it happen, just like in that movie or song. Why is that? With more than 50 percent of marriages ending in divorce, we know that living "happily ever after" is just a fantasy. As we mature, have children, and face responsibilities we didn't even know about when we took our marriage vows, we realize there is much more to making love work than we naively imagined at that altar.

It's astounding how many people get married with little to no idea of what they are doing or why. If only we could take some of the effort and money we spend on planning a wedding and allocate it for premarital counseling, the world would be a better place. Preparing for any major life-changing event should be required, but the thought of doing this rarely occurs to people—except those who ascribe to the essential codes of the Catholic religion. They make it mandatory for couples taking their vows to attend premarital classes. If only we could make it a federal law, especially for first-timers! If only someone would tell all these gullible young men and women that their marriage is not going to play out like a Disney movie!

I've certainly tried with several clients, but I guess they need to fall on their own, as a toddler might do on their first day in a new playground.

If only it were that innocent.

Harassment usually begins at home, and it comes in many shades. It can be physical, emotional, verbal, sexual, intellectual, or spiritual. Children who grow up in homes where harassment is a lifestyle will assume that it is the norm and mimic this behavior as they mature. When children are subjected to their mother being judged, criticized, or abused, they will either identify with the abuser or the victim, but neither one is a healthy choice. Sons will often model their fathers, while girls copy their mothers.

This often becomes multigenerational behavior until a therapeutic intervention can interrupt the cycle. In *Healing the Shame that Binds You*, author John Bradshaw explains how multigenerational shame fosters each generation's behavior until somebody breaks the cycle.

To be fair, some women are attracted to or even addicted to power. They seek out the attention of "strong" men for their aggrandizement. These predatory women pursue men of power to gain power of their own and are willing to sell their souls to the devil to accomplish it.

The quintessential femme fatale, Scarlett, from Gone with the Wind, used every man who could provide for her and satisfy her demands. She was ruthless, even stealing her sister's fiancé to secure lumber to rebuild Tara. Hers is a universal archetype and can be observed in every era and culture. Rita Hayworth portrayed this archetype in Gilda in the early forties. She represented a beautiful woman seeking a powerful man to empower herself.

The Cost of Addiction

I have met countless women in my practice who are not unlike cocaine addicts in their efforts to find more powerful men with each new conquest, willing to pay any price to land their man. As far as I can see, the cost always outweighs the gain. Men attracted to this archetypal female will invariably find younger and prettier choices. For many of these women, the high from conquering a man of power is worth the pain.

How does this begin? These conquests come from a lack of self-esteem, low self-worth, and the search for finding a way to believe that they matter. Beneath this persona is usually a lost, wounded child looking for love in all the wrong places. Healthy, evolved women would not be attracted to this kind of man. They hold themselves to a higher standard while exemplifying a strong sense of self, dignity, and self-respect. They would reject coupling with a man just to feel worthy as a woman. It's a matter of values and integrity.

Women use their sexuality to gain power in the same fashion that men use their pocketbooks to conquer women. Like many addictions, this cycle usually becomes progressive and pervasive.

Margie's Myth

Margie plowed through powerful men like a bull in a china shop. Each conquest was a trophy, earning her the best that life had to offer, as well as the worst. By the time she was fifty, Margie had struggled through three divorces, two live-ins, and two prominent, successful boyfriends, all of whom lied and cheated. She had a knack for picking these guys out.

When she came into my office, she was with the last of these predatory men. Each had poked a bigger hole in her soul than the last. When she revealed their abusive behavior, I asked her why she allowed them to treat her in such an unflattering and degrading manner. Her answer was common. I have heard it many times from the partners of drug addicts and alcoholics. "When he's not fuckin' around, he's wonderful. He treats me like a queen. He took me to Europe three times this year. He bought me expensive designer clothes, two Prada bags, and much more. We're perfect for each other. We get along great, and we have fun."

In Margie's case, it was the cheating that drove her mad.

"I give him my whole self. I am a great lover. We have amazing sex. I even suck his toes as well as his cock. We fall into each other's arms, embracing each other with repeated lovemaking. Then, the drama begins. He gets up to go to the bathroom in the middle of the night and texts some other chick about their next rendezvous. I see it on his phone every morning. It's almost as if he leaves it for me to uncover."

"Really?" I've heard this before from other women, but I'm still astonished.

"How long has this been going on?"

"From the beginning, for the entire four years we've been together. I discovered it early. He has many women all over the world that he uses for sex and entertainment. He says it means nothing. It's just recreation for him, like gambling or spending a day at the races."

"How do you feel when you realize he has all these other women?"

"Terrible, like I don't mean that much to him. It makes me crazy and fills me with rage. One time, I actually pushed him into his closet and attacked him, punching him wherever my fist would land. I literally beat him up. I felt like I turned into a she-devil, which I'm really not, and I didn't like myself at all."

"Then why are you with him? What's your payoff or secondary gain for staying with someone who spends time with other women?"

Margie's story is sadly familiar. She is willing to lose her self-worth, self-respect, and dignity to keep this relationship alive. On top of that, she's putting herself at risk for a plethora of venereal diseases. But she won't let go. For her, the pleasure is worth the pain. The highs cancel the lows. Each new conquest might double its value while each one that ends becomes more costly to her self-esteem. These patterns are eerily similar to most addictions, and the behavior this requires is generated by the unconscious.

Margie is one of many I have counseled. When working through these case studies, the common denominator is always the same: low self-worth, shame, and early childhood wounds from abuse, neglect, or abandonment. In Margie's case, she decided long before she became an adult that she would never be poor again. The economic struggles she encountered in her childhood gave rise to her addiction to abusive men. But it wasn't as simple as that. Her father's failures to secure her childhood safety also contributed to her choices as an adult. The specific content is different in each case. Still, there is an underlying feeling of not feeling good enough for various reasons, each having to do with unresolved familial issues, and most of it is triggered by fathers or another dominant male.

It is well-known that little girls get their self-worth from their daddies. It's part of the developmental process. When this doesn't happen, girls grow up looking for what was missing when they were children: the need to feel they mattered and the need to feel safe and secure. They act out their feelings in their adult life with a recapitulation to the past buried deep inside them. The resolution resides in treatment—and not in a man.

Beyond Money

Some women are attracted to powerful men for their status and accomplishments rather than just their bank accounts. These men are often well-respected pillars in the community—politicians, clergy, professors, and humanitarians. They appear to be virtuous, honorable men that no one would suspect had a bad bone in their body.

In Woody Allen's *Crimes and Misdemeanors*, Judah Rosenthal is a pious Jew, philanthropist, and philanderer, a man of high character and morals who also happens to be chief of ophthalmology at a large hospital on Long Island. To honor him for his outstanding service to the community, the hospital is dedicating a new ophthalmology center in his name. As the movie unfolds, we learn that Judah, who is married and planning his daughter's wedding, is not such a nice guy. He's been having an affair with a flight attendant, who, after a few years, insists that he leave his wife and make a life with her. Her nagging and persistence make Judah more and more uncomfortable. He tries to reason with her, console her, and make her understand that a divorce is not possible. Unable to control her demands and outbursts, he hires a hit man through a sleazy network connected to his shady brother. The murder is committed and goes unresolved. After struggling with overwhelming shame and guilt, Judah eventually continues his life as if the killing never happened. His wife and daughter never find out, and his peers and colleagues maintain the belief that he is a man of substance, held in high regard by his colleagues and the community. Woody Allen portrays the dark side of a man of piety and honor. In some ways, he may have been portraying the shadowy side of himself.

Women pursuing so-called honorable men are usually bright, well-educated, and successful in their careers, but they are also seeking mental and intellectual stimulation, which means they need men who imbibe many of the same moral qualities and religious values they possess. These women often meet a Dr. Jekyll and soon learn that the man's alter ego, his Hyde, is lurking in the shadows of the man they thought matched their standards.

This is not to say that men are exempt from this unexpected deception. They can be duped by unscrupulous women too, but most men don't stick around if that becomes clear. Some do, however, and in that case, most hope they will see a change in the woman's behavior over time.

Generally, women are more patient and understanding than men. As men sit, "pinned and wriggling on the wall," as T.S. Eliot wrote in *The Love Song of J. Alfred Prufrock*, they are more of a challenge than women when it comes to breaking down defenses and opening up to communicate in a genuine, meaningful way. At least, that has been my experience.

Character defects linger without therapeutic intervention and sometimes never disappear, even with it, because the payoff is too great to make any change. All too often, men are willing to lose the woman in exchange for their character defect. For them, it's just an addiction, with the drug of choice being conquering women. What remains so baffling is that so many of these accomplished, intelligent women continue to stick it out with these objectionable men.

Sarah's Lament

One day, a beautiful, bright, and successful fifty-four-year-old woman entered my office. Sarah had been in a rocky relationship with a man of power for nearly eight years. During their time together, he clarified that marriage or cohabitation would never happen. He made the rules, and she sadly capitulated. It hadn't been like that in the beginning, though.

"The first night we met, there were fireworks. We were introduced by a colleague of Sam's, and the chemistry was off the charts. Sam couldn't wait to spend nights with me. On the second night after we met, he said, 'I want to get this right!' He wined and dined me and took me to Italy only two months after we met. We shopped in the finest boutiques. He bought me beautiful clothes and fine jewelry and totally swept me off my feet. He introduced me to Italian art and all his favorite painters. I felt like a princess and fell madly in love. After we returned home, he placed a bottle of wine we had brought back from Rome on his kitchen counter. 'When you are certain,' he said, 'we'll open this and celebrate our commitment.'"

Sarah looked down while sharing her story. She was tearing up, heartbroken, in deep despair, and in disbelief that their relationship had so swiftly dissipated into mere dreams. She realized that she had allowed it to linger to a point that was way past due. Once the conquest was over, her knight in shining armor morphed into the exact type of person she had been trying to avoid.

Sam became the jerk she never would have suspected. He disconnected, slowly but surely, pulling away each time he chose to go off and play golf, ride a bike, or partake in an activity that didn't include Sarah. She had walked away five times during their relationship, only to surrender to his wishes each time he made an overture to reconcile. Each reunion would last less than a year before the same behavior reared its ugly head again.

"Nothing changes until it changes," she told me. "I felt like I was in a merry-go-round relationship. I would have these heart-to-heart talks with Sam. He would be conciliatory, never defending his behavior, and then he would apologize before we parted. A few months would pass, and I would hear from him again as if nothing had happened. It was so crazy."

Sam was a renowned neurosurgeon and author, one reason Sarah was so attracted to him, and he traveled more than he stayed home. Born and raised in Santiago, Chile, until he was fifteen, Sam became a star soon after his family settled in Chicago. His good looks and Latin accent made him irresistible to the opposite sex, and with age, he became even more appealing. He excelled in everything. He was president of his high school class, a four-letter athlete, and a scholar. His power did not stem from money. It was spawned from fame and endless charm.

Sarah told me that Sam was the most intelligent man she had ever known, a sort of Renaissance man interested in art, literature, fine wine, writing, and medicine. He would hold court in social settings, and since he was such an authority on brain disorders, everyone was spellbound when he spoke. He was invited all over the world to lecture at medical conferences. He introduced Sarah to many things she had rarely encountered. She had been grateful for each experience he shared. However, their traveling dwindled to occasional vacations, with him always choosing the destination, as he was rarely interested in where she wanted to visit.

I asked her why she stayed in the relationship once she realized they didn't want the same things, when it became clear that her needs were not being met. Her pain was palpable.

"Honestly, I don't know. It's an addiction or codependency. I guess they're the same. I can't call it love, but I can't seem to let him go, and he feels the same. Clearly, he's not in love with me. Sam has never told me that he loves me. When I ask if he missed me when he's been away, he always replies, 'No. I don't miss you when I'm gone. I have too many things to distract me, but I enjoy you when we are together.' I don't understand why I continue to ask him the same question, as if he will change his answer. He has never introduced me to anyone as his girlfriend or significant other. I am always introduced as 'just Sarah' or 'Oh, this is Sarah.' It's so insulting and humiliating. It makes me feel as if I don't matter. We haven't had sex in over a year. Sam says it's his prostate. He doesn't even kiss me or touch me. Occasionally, he takes my hand in a movie. He never looks into my eyes. He's hardly present. I can't believe I've settled for a loveless relationship. I could accept his diminished libido, but it's so painful to be deprived of closeness and connection. I have asked myself the same question many times. I find myself cursing when he turns everything around and blames me. My response is always muffled by his words and tone. Sam talks over me, and I feel stupid and dismissed. I hang up the phone, spewing, 'Fuck you!' He brings the worst out in me, and I don't like it. It's not who I am!"

"Then what keeps you in the relationship? It's not the money. You do well on your own."

"After eight years, it's become the norm, a habit I can't break. The pain must be worth the pleasure. Sam's a nice guy. He spends time talking to people all over the world he has never met who have a brain tumor or some neurological disease. They search him out, and he feels good when he helps others. He is nice to everyone—waiters, bellhops, children, animals. It's difficult to see the Hyde in him when he's Dr. Jekyll. It feels like eight years of my life have been wasted. I met Sam when I was forty-six, and I'm fifty-five. What the hell is wrong with me?"

Sarah began to sob.

"That was the way it was until it wasn't. One day, he accidentally left his phone at my home. It rang, and I picked it up by responding, 'This is Sam's phone.' The caller abruptly hung up, but the screen showed a woman's name and a city in another state. Moments later, a text arrived with a message that sent chills up my spine. A wave of nausea ran through me. Her message was a sex text, wondering when they could get together again. When I confronted Sam, he apologized, denying that he had ever participated. He said she was someone from the past he had not seen in years, a nurse who assisted him in the operating room. He asked for forgiveness, swearing it never happened, and he would not respond to any more communication she initiated. Foolishly, I accepted his apology."

I waited for her to go on, pretty sure that it hadn't ended right then and there.

"But it didn't stop!" Sarah said. "It kept going, and I could not accept this behavior. After the second time, I realized I had no choice but to end it. I had too much evidence to stay in denial. I reminded him about a quote, which was so apropos. "Fool me once, shame on you. Fool me twice, shame on me." Anyway, somehow, deep inside me, my soul would not rest unless I let go. I had lost respect and trust—for him, of course, but for myself too. There was no way in hell I could maintain a relationship with a liar and a cheater."

Unlike Margie, Sarah felt being alone would be preferable to chronic disappointment. She didn't want to wake up each morning facing the truth about her hollow relationship. The ups were no longer worth the downs. The payoff was no longer worth the pain. Sarah reclaimed her self-worth and moved on with dignity.

Gabby Makes a Deal

A young, beautiful widow named Gabby came to see me. She and her two teenage children had been left with little money from her husband's death. He had committed suicide, and his life insurance policy denied them any benefits. She took a job in sales in an exclusive department store, selling fine jewelry. She struggled to meet her debts and lived month to month until she met a man named Umberto.

One evening, while attending a musical at a local theater, Gabby was immediately attracted to the conductor, whose passion and sensual expressions instantly commanded her heart. Immediately after the performance, Gabby found her way backstage to meet the man who had captivated her when he lifted his arms to conduct the first notes of Jesus Christ Superstar. Umberto was Italian, with all the accoutrements common to handsome men of that heritage, especially a conductor showing such leadership and command.

That night began a romance that would last more than twenty-seven years.

Umberto traveled worldwide, conducting *Jesus Christ Superstar* with a traveling troupe, along with additional cast members he auditioned wherever they performed. Gabby went with him, attending most of his performances, and because Umberto had accrued a surplus of miles, they usually flew first class. He moved into her apartment soon after her children went to college. Umberto paid half of her rent and absorbed half the living expenses, even though he was living there less than half the time.

Gabby's life had become economically secure but at a high price. Umberto was a womanizer. Wherever he conducted, women were seduced by his charm, his accent, and his talent. They leaped at the chance to go to bed with him, and he could not resist. He was the archetypal Don Juan and made no excuses to Gabby. They were his willful prey and there to stay.

"I was devastated," she said, in mourning. "I could not believe he had bedded so many women. I thought he was faithful and loved me. I never suspected he had someone wherever he performed. Worst of all, he never kept it hidden. It was as if he wanted me to know."

"How does that make you feel, knowing he has been with many other women?"

Gabby's response was no different from Margie's or Sarah's.

"Horrible! I feel like shit, like I'm just one of many, like a part of his harem. There is no exclusivity! I don't feel special, loved, or important."

"Are you willing to continue, knowing there are other women wherever he travels?"

Gabby didn't answer.

"Do you realize that in addition to chronic emotional pain, you are susceptible to venereal disease?"

She seemed to skip over my last question. "I'm sure he is careful," she said.

I found her reply curious. "Well, what's good for the goose is good for the gander," she said. "I can play the same game as him."

"Well, that's an option, but what about your feelings? How will you negotiate them?"

"Ignore them," said Gabby. "I can have fun and find distraction just like him."

I saw her pain and sorrow. She was fighting back tears.

"Why would you want to choose that path? You are young, smart, and beautiful. You can find another man who can make you feel like you matter. Every time you are confronted with another betrayal, your heart breaks a little more, and that impacts your self-esteem. Life is too short to hang around men who suck the happiness out of you. You can do better, Gabby!"

"You don't understand. I have a great life with Umberto. We have unbelievable sex. All my expenses are covered. I travel the world first class, and he is so exciting. I suppose the turn-on is worth the pain."

"Worth your broken heart and self-esteem?" I said. "Think about it. You are suffering from unrequited love. It's a prescription for pain."

"What kind of man am I going to find out there?" said Gabby. "All men are dogs, right?"

I remained neutral, for professional and personal reasons.

"I know it's a bargain, but I don't see a better one out there. I believe Umberto loves me, but it's love on his terms. It's the best he can do."

"Then, why come to therapy? It sounds like you have made your decision."

"I needed someone outside of my friends and family to talk to. I don't tell my family anything. They don't need to know, and I don't share this with my kids. "

"Think about how they would respond if they knew."

"That's why I don't want them to know. I want to share it with someone who won't judge me, a person I can trust, like you. I didn't realize I would come to this conclusion on my own."

A few months later, Gabby opted for the deal she got from Umberto. I told her that if she wanted to stay in the relationship, she would have to accept the conditions and not allow his infidelity to break her heart. It was a deal made with the devil, but many women have pulled it off, although I challenge how successfully. There's always a downside. If a woman can handle it, she should stop complaining and move on. The right to self-determination is always a choice.

While this relationship would be untenable for some, it was

worth it to Gabby. She viewed the compromises she had to make and the pain and heartbreak she endured as a fair trade for the twenty-seven years they stayed together. A few months after she terminated treatment with me, Gabby passed away from lung cancer. I remain convinced that the relentless stress and intractable grief may have been her executioner.

Angela's Ashes

One of the most tragic cases I have ever encountered involves a woman named Angela. Born and raised in the Midwest as the younger of two girls, Angela was held hostage by her father for forty-three years, initially programmed as a child to be his sex slave. She was too young to understand his reprehensible behavior, and she kept it a secret, as her father commanded her to do. He brainwashed her into believing that they had a special relationship and that it should be kept private between the two of them. Angela was obedient and subservient to his commands and wishes, and the secret stayed with her until she managed to escape at forty-three.

When Angela first came to therapy, she had no memory before the age of seventeen. She could not recall her father's sexual violations on her body that ultimately produced a dissociative disorder, along with stuttering. The silence he demanded through intimidation and obedience resulted in submissive behavior in all her relationships. Silence became her default persona, while an internal rage damaged her spirit and self-worth. She had been allowed to attend school, but her father commanded Angela to return directly home when the final bell rang, preventing her from normal school activities and friends. Her social life was nonexistent.

Despite her father's control and confinement, Angela developed a strong interest in and talent for Tai Chi. Ironically, she was encouraged and supported by her father. She won many local, state, and national competitions. It was her passion for Tai Chi that perhaps saved her life and sublimated her rage. Her father chaperoned her trips and managed her schedule. Her mother stood by like a ghost, denying the sexual assaults perpetrated by her husband on their daughter.

For forty-three years, they lived in silent violence, each afraid to acknowledge their family secrets. Soon after Angela's older sister found her way out of the household and shared that she too had been sexually assaulted by their father since early childhood, Angela finally escaped.

I sat in my chair, horrified and in disbelief. I had heard about kidnappings and children being forced to have sex with their captors, but I had never heard of a story like Angela's. Desperate to find a semblance of recovery, and without even meeting me in person, she had taken a huge chance and traveled a great distance to embark on this journey with me, as she wanted to see someone experienced in inner child work. She had escaped her home and left the torture behind her, but it had followed her for another twelve years. At fifty-five, she showed up in my office.

Angela was deeply shattered by the wounds her father had inflicted, and now she was on the edge of ending a relationship with a man. For five intensive days and nights, we hammered out her past. It took several days for her to recall instances in her early childhood where her father had forced her to have sex with him. She was just a child, five years old, when he first fondled her body and had her open her legs so he could put his finger into her vagina. He forced her to suck his penis, telling her that a child who loves her daddy would want to make him happy like that, so he forced her little mouth around it until he would get an erection and ejaculate. Angela confessed that although this made her very uncomfortable, she enjoyed the feeling of him performing on her. Because she was so embarrassed to share her sexual arousal, she sobbed with guilt and shame.

The more Angela shared her daunting past, the more she remembered. The rage she had been holding inside for so long was manifesting itself in her relationship with her lover, which meant that both of them were suffering the consequences of her past. The further we probed, the more her soft demeanor morphed into a raging bull. She screamed for the child she had left behind. She actually gave her lost child a voice, one she was never allowed to have.

As she crouched on her knees on a mat in my office, she held a bat over her head and stared frozen at the large pillows on the floor.

"I can't do this. I can't hit my father. Please, is there another way?"

"Bring it down on the pillow," I urged. "Put your father on the pillow and say what you couldn't say when you were young and helpless. Tell him he stole your childhood and took away your innocence."

She sat motionless with the bat above her head, unable to bring it down.

"Give him back the shame he gave you. Bring it down. He's right there!"

I continued to bellow these instructions while pointing to the pillow. It took some time, but finally, after hearing my voice in the background urging her to take back her life and give him back the shame that didn't belong to her, she took the plunge.

At first, the bat came down softly, too hesitant to project her childhood voice and demeanor.

"More force! Just hit the pillow a few times and imagine he is coming into your room and sliding beside you in your bed. Reclaim your child! Save her!"

Angela stared at the pillow, holding the bat over her head. Then, she shrieked the words she could never say as a child. Even as she developed into a teenager and a young woman, she had no voice—not until now, in my office. She let loose, and once those words were unconstrained, she was no longer bound by fear or shame. Her voice penetrated the office walls, bursting through time and space, freeing her from her past's physical, emotional, and spiritual bondage.

"I hate you! You destroyed my life, you scumbag, son of a bitch, piece of shit. How dare you! You took away my childhood. You stole my innocence, you bastard. I hate you!"

Angela howled on and on, cursing her father over and over, heaving, nearly breathless, pounding the bat with foreign energy and force. She unleashed her locked-in-her-belly rage.

After each episode and outburst, I placed a teddy bear in her arms, symbolizing her inner child, and provided her with the words that had been denied to her as a child—words that would provide her with a validation she had never experienced.

"It's not your fault, Angela. It's not your fault."

She muttered the words softly to the teddy bear.

"You were precious, perfect, lovable, and innocent—a child of God."

Once again, she repeated my words.

"It wasn't your fault."

They seemed to stick with her for a minute before she could repeat them.

"You didn't deserve this, Angela, and from now on, I am going to take care of you."

She looked at me, and I nodded, a silent reminder that she was her own ultimate caretaker.

"I will take care of you forever, and of all the people you will meet, I am the one who will never abandon you."

Tears fell as Angela heard her words, and she repeated them as they began healing her soul. She supplemented them with her own to help her inner child heal from the years of wounds inflicted upon her by her father.

The wounds of a child remain until a corrective experience occurs. Although the treatment was demanding and painful, it had to be done. By breaking through the wall of repression and amnesia to discover her truth, Angela was finally on her way. I encouraged her to write her story, to make it known to others who had experienced a similar traumatic injustice. Eventually, she self-published a book, leading to her psychological and spiritual freedom.

Abuse in Common

In her book *The Drama of the Gifted Child*, Alice Miller writes that it is not just the action alone that makes us sick. It is the repression and secret that keep us from healing.

In ordinary, everyday relationships, we see power struggles, painful to both men and women. A healthy relationship is never based on power. It is egalitarian by nature. The power in a relationship exists in the relational space where the couple resides—not in one or the other. What makes the space healthy is being present and connected, seeing each other with new soft eyes and an open heart, and all the while learning the landscape and language of each other.

Margie, Sarah, Gabby, and Angela suffered from emotional and spiritual abuse. All were successful. Each earned a substantial amount of money. Margie believed it was never enough, caused by her insatiable childhood wound. Sarah felt her self-worth was more important than her legendary boyfriend. Gabby made herself a martyr and a victim. Angela was finally liberated.

Many women who are physically abused, battered, and sexually assaulted choose to stay in relationships, regardless of black eyes, broken bones, and scarred faces. Sleeping with the enemy is a common phenomenon in our culture. All are a love addiction. These women are addicted to their abuser due to low self-esteem and a fear of abandonment. Some fear leaving because of unimaginable consequences they can't seem to cope with or accept.

It is important to note that at least one in every three women worldwide has been beaten, coerced into sex, or otherwise abused during their lifetime. Most often, the abuser is a member of their own family. What seems most astounding is that according to the Violence Policy Center, each day in the United States, nearly three women are murdered by their husbands or boyfriends.

Except for Angela, all the other women were addicted and self-imprisoned by their captors—the men they chose as partners. None of them were victims. Margie, Sarah, and Gabby each had a choice. Angela was held hostage through intimidation and obedience.

The power was different in each man. Margie's partner had enormous wealth, Sarah and Gabby's partners had position and fame, and Angela had a commanding, controlling, and formidable father. Each woman capitulated to their oppressor for their own reasons. Each paid an enormous price. Angela, of course, had no options. Margie, Sarah, and Gabby each chose their partners unconsciously to teach them an important lesson they needed to learn.

Unfortunately, they didn't have the opportunity to work as a couple to discover the lesson and reap its benefits. It takes both partners to commit to work through underlying issues. However, individually, they could see that the fantasy they projected did not match reality. Each chose their fate based on whether the consequences were worth it for them.

Perhaps these women could have benefited from *Hamlet*, as written by William Shakespeare.

> "To be, or not to be, that is the question:
> Whether 'tis nobler in the mind to suffer
> The slings and arrows of outrageous fortune,

Or to take arms against a sea of troubles,
And by opposing end them? To die: to sleep;
No more; and by a sleep to say we end
The heart-ache and the thousand natural shocks
That flesh is heir to, 'tis a consummation
Devoutly to be wish'd. To die, to sleep;
To sleep: perchance to dream: ay, there's the rub:"

What Do We Do Now?

Relationship work is a process, not a one-time event. It needs to be taught and integrated; there is no handbook when we fall in love. When learning an instrument, to play a sport, to drive a car, etc., there are lessons. Some require a test to pass before you indulge. Yet, marriage and parenting, perhaps the most important investments we make, require no litmus test. Wouldn't a course in making love work be a good idea? Perhaps a course in "The Power of the Penis, the Patriarchy, Politics, and the Pocketbook" would do many women—and men—a lot of good.

The most common way people give up their power is by thinking they don't have any.

—ALICE WALKER

Chapter Four

The Dangers, Drags, and Dubious Dregs of the Dating Game

DATING IN THE twenty-first century is not for sissies! Consider yourself lucky if you're not stuck in that chaos, but if you are, keep reading! The dating world can be disastrous, but when a relationship grows and you become fully invested in a guy, what do you do when he suddenly decides he wants out?

"It's not about you; it's about me!"

Sound familiar?

Of course, this comment is even worse when your man goes MIA in a marriage or long-term relationship, but even in the context of dating, it can be debilitating. When you confront your partner with feelings of abandonment or detachment, what does he do? He either denies his behavior, which makes you feel like you're crazy, or he fesses up, admitting that he's not feeling the way he felt when your relationship began.

You ask yourself, "Is it me? Have I changed? What have I done wrong?" You tell yourself you are the same person you were a year ago, except a year older. Confused and bewildered, you second-guess yourself and develop a sudden case of insecurity and a new set of feelings that you no longer matter. "What did I have then that I don't have now?" The worst part is, you'll probably be on your own to answer these questions because Mr. It's Not About You; It's About Me will be long gone. In that case, stop blaming yourself and choose to not be a victim, especially not because of him.

The Bait and Switch, the Hit-and-Run, and the Seven-Year Itch Versus the Seven-Week Dude

In relationships, these terms have different meanings than the common dictionary definitions.

Hit-and-run is used primarily in auto accidents, but it can be easily applied to the dynamics of a relationship, particularly in its beginning stages.

Bait and switch is a form of fraud commonly used in retail sales when customers are baited by merchants advertising products or services at a low price, but when customers visit the store or website, they discover that the advertised goods are not available, or the customers are pressured to consider similar but higher priced items. This term also describes what happens during the first stage of a relationship.

Picture this: you think you've met a terrific man, but then you turn the corner, and without warning, out comes his polar opposite. You've suddenly entered the world of Dr. Jekyll and Mr. Hyde. In the beginning, Dr. Jekyll presents himself as a charming, well-intended potential partner. He's present, asks the right questions, and showers you with affirming comments, making you feel that he is genuinely interested in getting to know you. His gentle kiss when you say goodnight leaves you with a warm, fuzzy feeling, and when he says let's do this again or promises that he'll call, it sounds real, so you go home filled with excitement and hope—until he never calls, and you're left alone to wonder why.

For years, I have heard numerous women tell me similar stories of dating disasters, some of which took a long time to manifest.

As we know, things can often look rosy in the beginning, during the honeymoon phase, before other realities set in. Here are a few examples of the follies of our so-called "meaningful" relationships.

Janice and Alex

They were introduced through a mutual friend when she was fifty-eight and he was fifty-nine, but neither knew the other's age. The moment they met, Alex showered Janice with compliments, which were soon followed by promises. He played her like a Stradivarius, enticing her into his larger-than-life existence. Strangely, Alex never asked her age, although he later admitted that he believed Janice to be in her forties. Janice, beguiled by Alex's methods of seduction, fell deeply in love with him and the lifestyle he offered. He convinced her to move into his 8,500 sq. ft. mansion on the water overlooking Biscayne Bay, one of the most exclusive neighborhoods in Miami Beach. No home in that area was worth less than ten million dollars. Wide-eyed and bushy-tailed, she accepted his offer.

A successful professional, Janice took a leap of faith and was persuaded by Alex to sell her apartment, which she did before moving into his home, believing that "This is it. I've finally found my one true love!" She had endured two failed marriages and a few long-term relationships, including a five-year, live-in affair. At this point in her life, Janice was no novice. One would think that an intelligent, self-made woman would have given up on the fantasy of finding a dream man. But like many bright, middle-aged women only six years away from Medicare, fantasy can still trump reality, and the lure of the Disney prince still reigns, at least enough to make women like Janice sell their home and move in with a man they don't know very well. She was blissfully unaware that she was selling her soul to the devil. Janice lost herself in the promises of a man she knew for less than six months.

Alex had been married twice, had two grown children who

lived on their own, and appeared totally smitten with Janice—until the day she announced that her son and daughter-in-law were going to have a baby, making her a grandma for the first time. It was then, coupled with their first international trip, that Alex discovered Janice's real age. In no time, he began to withdraw from their relationship. It was subtle at first, but she soon felt him become more and more distant and wondered what had caused the shift. When she confronted him about her feelings, he dismissed it as untrue and blamed it on her insecurities. Alex never admitted his disappointment with her age and that she would soon have a grandchild. He pretended to keep the relationship alive, but all the while, he was having an affair, unbeknownst to Janice, who still believed he was faithful and in love with her.

It didn't take much longer before Alex's behavior morphed into estrangement and aggression. He no longer showered Janice with compliments. He became hostile and easily irritated without cause or provocation. Their once-fulfilling sex life became much less satisfying, bordering on barren. When Janice tried to communicate her feelings, Alex stonewalled her, which made her feel intimidated and unable to express herself. Confused, bewildered, and rejected, she continued to believe that their relationship was intact and that perhaps Alex had been correct in his interpretations regarding her insecurities.

Self-doubt and suspicion soon replaced contentment and joy.

By then, Janice and Alex had lived together for nearly three years, traveling and maintaining social engagements. Alex had several personal and business issues that infiltrated their relationship, contaminating what was once their sacred space. Janice tried to support his concerns with her twenty-five years of experience as a psychologist, but her words fell on deaf ears. The more she tried to console him, offering suggestions and viable options, the more defensive and combative he became. Alex's judgments, fault-finding, and criticism became pervasive. Then, one Tuesday evening, he told Janice he had not been happy for a year and wanted her to leave, giving her until that Friday to get out.

Janice was stunned. She was clueless about what had happened to cause such a sudden dismissal. She confessed that she had been aware of the shift in their connection but didn't realize he had been so unhappy. Alex had disguised his feelings so well that she was shocked to learn that he had not been happy for an entire year. They had just returned from a great weekend with friends and her family. Janice assumed it was the stress Alex was feeling from his business and his daughter, who had always felt contempt for him due to unresolved childhood issues.

To Alex's wishes, Janice moved out. A friend offered her an apartment until she found her own. Overwhelmed with grief and unexpected loss, Janice fell ill, and a broken heart soon morphed into diabetes. Her life had been shattered, along with her self-esteem. She was approaching sixty-two, alone, and essentially homeless. She never suspected that on Saturday, just one day after she left Alex's mansion on North Bay Road, another (younger) woman would move into what had been Janice's safe haven, abruptly taking over her closet and enjoying the furnishings and housewares Janice had chosen to create the home she and Alex had shared.

As soon as she heard about this, Janice made an appointment to see me. After listening to her story, I told her about another person I had treated for something similar.

Mindy and Jack

The night Mindy and Jack met through a mutual friend felt like a time warp for both of them. Mindy, a bright and beautiful woman in her late fifties, and Jack, a few years older but not yet retired, felt an instant mutual attraction.

"I want to get this right!" he told her on their second date the next night.

"Me too," Mindy said.

She was full of the same high hopes she once had with her first love many years earlier.

They both agreed not to jump between the sheets until they learned more about one another. It wasn't long before their hearts melded, and they were off to Italy to celebrate Mindy's sixtieth birthday.

Jack was an investment banker who had raised his two children as a single parent. His ex-wife had been determined to remain incompetent, leaving him with sole custody of their children. His work took him worldwide, making it difficult to manage fatherhood and a career. Both had been sacrificed along the way, but despite his time constraints and traveling, his children grew up to become successful adults and were his pride and joy.

When Jack met Mindy, he had quite a full life. In addition to his consulting work, he had written several books on the art of business and investment counseling and was amid more. He was well-respected and world-renowned in his field. He loved the arts, theater, ballet, concerts, and opera. Like Sam, the renowned neurosurgeon, Jack might also be considered a Renaissance man, which delighted Mindy to no end, just like Sarah with Sam. She fell head over heels for him, and he returned the affection, so she assumed he felt their relationship was "the real thing." He wined and dined her and couldn't get enough of her–physically and sexually.

Mindy thought she had won the lottery. In addition to all his charms, he was considerate, gracious, and generous, bestowing her with gifts she could never afford.

"I couldn't believe this man was for real. He was handsome, brilliant, humble, sexy, sophisticated, and worldly. I couldn't imagine what he might have seen in me. He was also philanthropic, great with my family, and loved to have fun. He played golf when he wasn't on a lecture tour and rode his bike for hours, sometimes as much as fifty miles. He swam as often as he could. I can't say enough about his character, which was authentic and good-natured from the start, until it slowly disappeared over the nine years we were together. Everything disappeared!"

Mindy's head fell into her hands as tears spilled down her cheeks, smearing her eyeliner and mascara. She took turns blowing her nose and pouring her heart out.

"Nine years!" she said. "Can you imagine? I was in a fucking trance for nine years—and I never did anything I knew that could have caused him to change his feelings and behavior. He pulled away slowly. I was so unsuspecting. It never occurred to me that he might be having an affair or that he even had an issue with me. He often found fault for the silliest reasons."

"Give me an example," I said. I wanted to understand Mindy's perception of silly.

"One time, when I asked for an umbrella in the rain, he became annoyed and criticized me for not wanting to get my hair wet. They were stupid reasons—the dumbest things—like putting on lipstick at the table in a restaurant or shaming me for wanting to get something to eat when I was hungry and he was entertaining his grandchildren. They were things I couldn't understand in the moment. It was as if he was trying to find reasons to withdraw. It worked, though, because his words of devotion and affection changed from 'You are loved and adored' or 'You are precious' to nothing. Zilch. He no longer said he loved me, and when I asked him if he missed me when he was away, he said, 'Well, now that you mention it, I like the solitude. It gives me time to think.' My heart sank. It was clear that he no longer wanted the relationship. We broke up six times during our nine years together, and he always took the initiative to come back to me. It was like a dance. 'Come here. No, go away.' I never knew how he really felt. Our lovemaking stopped completely, and when I tried to talk to him about it, I got one-word responses."

Mindy wiped her eyes, swollen and red, and leaned back.

"What's the use? It's done. He's gone and is probably relieved. His first intentions faded over time as we grew closer. I guess he was just another dude afraid of intimacy."

I handed Mindy another box of tissues. I had heard this monologue innumerable times and learned to keep a full supply of Kleenex in my office. In this case, Mindy's details differed from Janice's, but the structure always remained the same.

It was a dance of codependency. I call it the "come here, go away" two-step. I have counseled countless women who share the same heartbreak. My office had soaked up thousands of tears over the years. They cry me a river with their heartbreaking stories of disappointment and unwarranted rejection, and most never see the train coming, let alone the wreckage. Understanding their shortcomings and fears of intimacy never seems to matter to these women. Hit-and-run or bait and switch produce emotional effects that leave deep wounds, often requiring years of recovery. The scars can be triggered during future relationships, leaving people with post-traumatic stress disorder, including on dating sites.

A broken heart with broken dreams has no intellect or wisdom. It resides in the limbic system, only feeling pain and loss.

Mindy's parting words that day have stayed with me for a long time. She was the one who inspired the title of this book when she said, "I hate him. I hate that bastard! I hate the man I love, and I don't know what to do about it."

Seven-Week (Weak) Men

We cannot discuss the debacles of dating and relationships without including the "seven-week (weak) men" syndrome. During the entire span of my private practice, this theme has kept reappearing: women meeting men, online or otherwise, beginning a relationship with all the makings of success, only to have it end abruptly at the seven-week mark.

This is not too different from the "seven-year itch," when people (mostly men) seek a relationship outside their existing one at around the seven-year mark. Seven-week men check out after the conquest is confirmed, which usually takes place just short of two months. Some of these men are married, looking for a distraction from their boring marriage, while others are surfing for a short tryst to satisfy their sexual needs, but those urges seem to fade within seven weeks. Others may wig out when they realize that the woman they have "conquered" has fallen in love and expects a real commitment, something that never seems to occur to the man involved, from the get-go to the end. For most, if not all, of these men, the fling was only meant to satisfy their ego because conquering a woman always seems to make them feel more powerful.

Millie and Jason

These two met in a Whole Foods market. The moment they laid eyes on each other, sparks flew. It was as if they had known each other from a different lifetime.

"He was smitten from the moment our eyes met," Millie told me.

"What happened to suddenly change things?"

"I really don't know. Something in him, for sure, because he made plans to take me out for my birthday and brought several gifts. He said I looked beautiful, and then he kissed me and brought me close to him, telling me how much he loved me. 'There is something I need to tell you, Millie. This is not easy, and I know it will hurt you, but I can't see you anymore.' I freaked out. 'What?' I was shouting, which is out of character for me, but he shocked me. 'Seriously?' I said. 'You're joking, right?' Jason didn't say a single word. He just hunched over me while I sat frozen on the sofa. 'Don't ask me to explain, Millie. I can't. It's not going to work for me. It's not you. I love you—you're special. You're a blessing for any man.'"

I listened to Millie, saddened that she was hardly the only woman who had been through something like this. I nodded for her to continue.

"I said, 'Jason, you can't even give me a reason?' I tried to hold my tears back. I was so sad, and I felt so angry and even had physical pain. I couldn't define the myriad of feelings that were shooting through me like a torpedo."

Weeks later, Millie still writhed in discomfort as she disclosed her heartbreak.

"Why would someone who claimed he loved me leave me so suddenly, without any cause or explanation? Why?"

I had no response to alleviate her pain, no answer that would make sense. Jason was not my client, so there was no reason to project my thoughts onto him. I am not a mind reader, but Millie's story was not new. I had heard it too many times—boy meets girl, they fall in love, boy leaves girl for little or no apparent reason, and girl falls apart. In many cases, the girl gets pregnant and has the child without sharing the information with the father, and the child grows up fatherless, forever wondering about the identity of their father. Sometimes, she chooses to abort and keeps that information to herself.

The cascade of emotions that flow through these women often leaves irreparable scars. When this becomes a pattern, it is imperative to understand why they feel attracted to a man who can't commit. Why do we unconsciously keep repeating the same choices? As I previously pointed out, Sigmund Freud called it "repetition compulsion," while Alice Miller refers to it as "the logic of absurdity." Whatever you choose to call it, this cycle is something to be reckoned with!

A woman has to explore why she does what she does.

Why Do We Keep Repeating the Same Mistakes?

Women need to understand that this behavior is not a coincidence but a pattern that keeps repeating itself as we try to work out unfinished business from the past. Where does this madness come from, and why? The reasons are plentiful, but the common denominator is childhood wounds. Since we choose our mates both consciously and unconsciously, we must examine the "why." Otherwise, change can never occur.

This is how multigenerational shame is passed on. The pattern of looking for love in all the wrong places continues, no matter what we call it, whether it's codependency, the most common label, or a simple combination of bad judgment, desperation, or plain old stupidity.

One of my favorite examples of the seven-week exploitation cycle was presented by Julie, who came to see me soon after she split from her boyfriend of exactly seven weeks. The way she presented the story could easily have been made into a short novel. Her experience left such a jolting impression that she wrote a story to turn it into a novel. She brought her meanderings, reflections, and thoughts into our session. She had a bound manuscript with her and completed the first part, titled *The Illusion of Love: An Internet Disaster*.

I wanted to hear every word, although reading eighty-nine pages would have taken too long. She shared the most salient parts so I could get an accurate impression of her experience. Julie was an excellent writer, and I was fascinated by her story and how she presented the information.

Sydney, sixty-five and married, was seeking excitement as a distraction from his compulsive workaholic nature. He and his wife were separated but married. She lived in Chicago while he was in Miami. His buddies told him about internet dating, which he didn't know much about.

"Technically, I'm married and really not available," he said.

"Well, you are alone, Syd," one of his friends said, "and it will give you a diversion from all your work. You don't have to get serious. Just have some fun."

Sydney was an intellectual person, a powerful entrepreneur, and a successful developer. He took up his friends' suggestion, believing it would be an innocuous, innocent sport just for his amusement. He had absolutely no intention or interest in developing a relationship with anyone.

Julie, on the other hand, a bright, beautiful, and rather innocent woman in her early sixties, was seriously looking for a relationship. She was divorced three times and had three grown children and five grandchildren. She was a successful recruiter for an investment company, had lived alone for several years, and was eager to find a life partner. She joined a dating site, hoping she might find an appropriate mate who could fill her needs and desires. One evening, quite late, Julie pulled into her driveway with a sense of weariness. She opened the gate to the courtyard, ignoring the cascading sounds of recycled water pouring endlessly from the statue of the Water Lady perched upon a Roman fountain. When she turned the key and opened her front door, Danny Boy, her twelve-pound Maltese, was overjoyed to see her. He jumped up against her and wiggled his tail until she picked him up and kissed him hello. After searching the refrigerator, she settled for a soda and pretzels and headed toward her office. Her day had been filled with complaints and endless calls. Julie was beginning to appreciate the peace and tranquility single life and solitude could offer, although being alone was not her first choice.

She slipped off her heels, sat in front of her computer, and checked to see if she had received any responses to her online dating profile. The new messages of interested suitors were so homogeneous that it was difficult to distinguish one from the other. Nothing original. Even worse, the men were unattractive or barely presentable. Several had no photos, and she hated that. How could anyone expect a response without a photo? Hers was there for the world to see. Quite uncharacteristically, Julie ignored them all, except the one without a photo.

> *Good evening, Lady Julie,*
>
> *I want to know what you ache for and if you dare to dream of meeting your heart's desire. I want to know if you will risk looking like a fool for love, for your dream, and for the adventure of being alive. We have a great deal in common and a fair amount of distinction from each other. Would you be willing to communicate and explore the avenues that beckon us to travel on together?*
>
> *Yours,*
> *Sydney*

Julie told me that she considered ignoring the message.

"After all," she said, "there was no photo, and worse yet, his brief profile revealed that he was separated. There was nothing else he offered. I had promised never to date 'never married' or separated men. I felt it was a sure bet for future problems. There was always the chance that their marriage could be reconciled, or they were online surfing for an interruption from their mundane life. On top of that, he mentioned nothing about himself, except that he was separated. It's amazing how an incomplete profile could have elicited a response from me like it did. I guess the mystery was seductive, especially after reading his first entry."

By then, tears rolled down Julie's cheeks, and I offered her some tissues. I couldn't help but relate to her. Many of my own love-life experiences matched hers. Naturally, I wanted to hear more. I was fully aware of my emerging countertransference, but I kept the session clean, just listening with great awareness.

Julie continued to read from her manuscript.

Dear Sydney,

Your email was titillating and seductive. I felt compromised by not being able to see your photo or learn more about you. Your profile is empty. You have the advantage of viewing both my photo and my profile. Yours is like a skeleton. How can you expect anyone to learn anything about you and decide if there's any common ground? Perhaps you might be willing to consider filling in the gaps.

Yours,
Julie

This communiqué went on for several weeks until they finally met. He referred to her as "Cinderella" in all his emails and began signing them as "Prince Froggie." He assured her that she would not be disappointed. His writing style sizzled for her, and she was off to the moon on gossamer wings, creating her future life with this exciting man, who continued to shower her with Robert Browning-esque poetry, luring her to finally accept a date after just three weeks.

Julie's hunch wasn't wrong. Sydney drove up in a new premiere Jaguar, and when he entered her home, he dazzled her with his looks and style. He was everything she had hoped he would be—brilliant, handsome, rich, and seemingly smitten with her.

What more could a woman want?

He opened the door of his "carriage." As Julie entered, Sydney pointed out a gift on her seat, a small box, perfectly wrapped. Julie felt excited, like a little girl. Her giddiness in relating the story made it sound like it was happening to me. I was absorbed and swept away. I could identify with it. How many times had I found someone who met my criteria and expectations, who had the same presentation, and then disappointed me profoundly as he disappeared like a ghost?

Julie was not the only client I could compare notes with—there have been many—but her presentation took me onto a wavelength, making me concentrate on being mindful and present as her counselor instead of a commiserating girlfriend, a distinction I have to remind myself.

As she opened the gift, she was paralyzed with excitement when she saw a Limoges statue of a prince dressed in full regatta, holding his arm out with a glass slipper. My mouth joined hers—fully agape. We were both sharing the same experience of wonder and delight.

For a few weeks, things took off, and Julie's heart was filled with love and excitement. Syd showered her with gifts and confessed how much he loved her and wanted to spend his life with her—until he didn't. The charade lasted seven weeks.

Syd introduced Julie to his business partner, and his office was filled with his art holdings, covering most of the walls. His developments were pervasive, from New York to California and Florida. Julie had fantasies of giving up work and living a life of luxury, as Syd had intimated. Her excitement was transcended by her love for this man who had swept her off her feet.

But exactly seven weeks from the day she received her first email, the dream ended abruptly, and the nightmare began. Syd came to Julie's home. They watched Frida, a movie that explores fidelity and loyalty. When it was over, so was their romance—terminated by Prince Froggie, as he realized he had taken things with Julie too far and had no way to escape.

Goodbye, Cinderella.

Julie's hopes, dreams, and expectations dissipated into thin air, along with the man she thought would be the one to take her to a castle, where they would live happily ever after.

"You would think that by now, at sixty-two, I would know better. It's time I give up the fantasy." I looked at Julie and nodded, but I also made the same decision for myself.

What Do We Do Now?

It's difficult to change the neural pathways created by Disney and movies we watched during childhood. They leave such an indelible mark. Our beliefs are formed early, and abandoning them is not easy. Our mirror neurons allow us to mimic good and bad ideas and values. Being raised to believe that "someday my prince will come" is nearly impossible to erase. It follows us, and thinking we have outgrown the influence is something we do at our own risk.

My advice? Enjoy the movies alone, with children or grandchildren, or on a date, but remember—it's a movie. It's not real life! The only prince who will show up in your life is animated, and the only horse you may encounter leaves shit behind him on the ground, so watch your step!

Love never dies a natural death.
It dies because we don't know
how to replenish its source.
It dies of blindness and errors
and betrayals.
It dies of illness and wounds;
it dies of weariness;
of withering, of tarnishings.

—ANAIS NIN

Chapter Five

Don't Fix It! Just Listen!

MEN SEEM TO assume that when a woman expresses a concern or statement, he is automatically responsible for fixing it. For example, if she says the air conditioner is on the blink, it immediately elicits a response of annoyance or anger.

"Why can't you take care of it? Why is it always my job?"

God knows why men respond to their female partners this way, when the issue is simply that the air conditioner is not working. Unfortunately, his response leaves her wondering why he looks so cross as he screws up his face and rolls his eyes.

"I called the service company," she'll say, "and they are coming out tomorrow."

This is just one example of how men respond to something that sounds like a request or a demand instead of simply declaring what is true.

Why do men feel obligated to fix the problem when all the woman wants is for him to listen and share in the reality of the situation? Men are not alone in this conflict. Women often respond the same way, although, in fairness, not nearly as often or as belligerently.

The Gift of Active Listening

Perhaps the reason for all the misunderstanding boils down to one simple fact: listening is a skill, a learning process that requires mindfulness and practice.

Effective communication begins with active listening and is perhaps the most essential ingredient in any successful, conscious relationship. Sadly, most couples also lack it and seem to take it for granted.

Most couples think talking trumps listening, which is not true. Learning how to be present and listen is paramount in any relationship. Men assume too often that when the woman does not intend or request something, his mind is free to wander.

I saw this firsthand while sitting beside a couple returning from their vacation. The woman was perusing through an airline magazine, filled with destinations the airline traveled.

"Look, Honey, this looks like a great vacation spot," she said.

Without any provocation or expectation, her husband responded in an angry tone.

"I just took you to Hawaii. We haven't even been flying for an hour, and now you want me to take you on another vacation?"

That was not what I heard his wife say nor could it have possibly been interpreted that way. However, that was the message received by her husband, and he responded defensively and aggressively for no reason. He instinctively interpreted her comment as an expectation to take her on another vacation when all she did was share a photo of a resort.

This is how the relational space between a couple can become polluted. Once this occurs, the woman responds defensively, which only causes her partner to become reactive, and once that happens, the space between them becomes uncomfortable. Each reacts to the discomfort until the shared space they cocreated and are struggling to occupy becomes dangerous. This often leads to heated conflict or mutual disconnect.

Here's the problem: if we don't know how to take responsibility for that shared space, we will unwittingly pollute it.

In her workshops, Hedy Schleifer teaches about three invisible connectors: relational space, crossing the bridge, and the encounter. I have applied her techniques to reconnect couples by cleansing their relational space. It is not a difficult process, but it requires a big fat "yes" from each partner to be successful. Both must be willing to learn the process.

The Art of Being Present

Jewish philosopher Martin Buber said each partner does not make up the relationship. It does not live in one or the other. It lives in the space between each other. He called this the "sacred space." It is also the playground for our children and our pets, and like children, they are affected by pollution.

Children feel their environment, which often leaves emotional scars as they grow. Pets naturally hide under the bed if a space remains polluted. Luckily, they can remove themselves from the tension. Children can't. They feel responsible or guilty that they cannot fix whatever is causing the polluted space. For couples to create and maintain a conscious relationship, they must know about the space and take responsibility for maintaining its sacred nature.

Schleifer says that when we don't know about the space, we unconsciously pollute it with a word, look, judgment, criticism, reaction, or dialogue. To understand our partners and appreciate and negotiate our differences, she says that we must learn about their neighborhood, meaning the world in which they personally live.

This takes curiosity! Paying attention! Being present!

Each partner lives in a different world, based on their history and experience. It is the responsibility of each to learn the language of the other and their perceptions, wounds, and stories.

Couples often live together for years without really knowing the essence of their partner. They may end up living lives of quiet desperation or a louder version of the same. Either way, they live in a disconnected state.

When these couples met, each was wearing their survival suits, the ones created early in childhood for adaptation and protection. John Bradshaw refers to the survival suit as the "false self" or the "adaptive self." When two parties in a relationship struggle, their authentic selves become tucked deeply within their façade, afraid to be exposed. The longer they stay in hiding, for fear of punishment or shame, the larger the survival suit becomes. To really know our partners, they must uncover their survival suit, which is not easy!

Our survival suit protected us when we were young and vulnerable. During our youth, we needed to adapt to survive the dysfunction in our families of origin. That's because every family is dysfunctional, to a greater or lesser degree. Conscious parenting was not something brought to our attention when many of us grew up. Parents often parent how they were parented, which can be troublesome.

Doing what comes naturally was not always healthy. As we grew older, the suit was no longer useful. It actually became counterproductive. After wearing it for so many years, we became accustomed to it, believing that the suit is really who we are. It is not.

Who we really are lies beneath the façade, which for some becomes rigid armor. We are not the suit. Our authentic self, our essence, lies within, and each person in a relationship must be present enough to pay attention to that and be curious enough to find out what is underneath. Only then can a relationship become truly interesting and thrive.

So, what do we do? Before we can listen by being fully present, we need to learn how to do it. This is not as easy as it sounds;

most of us are not used to being in this state of mind. There are too many distractions, always ready to interfere with staying present. Technology has transformed our lives, and not always in a good way. Phones ring, texts chime, messages ding, emails pile up, clients are demanding, children need attention, family and friends require the same, and exhaustion ensues. As a result, we have limited time and energy to take care of the space in our relationships, which is our most precious tenure. For many of us, our relationships are neglected until it's too late. Is it any wonder why more than 50 percent of marriages in the US end in divorce?

Relationships matter!

So, what is the art of being present? To be fully present for your partner, you must make time without any distractions; otherwise, it won't work. There is only so much time available to us. Our partners and children know if they are valued by the quality of time we spend with them. This is also true of aging parents we too often neglect.

We make time to have our hair cut, watch a movie, see sporting events, or listen to the news. We carve out the time to attend a concert, tend to our garden, work out at the gym, or hang out with friends and family, but we don't set aside time to just be with our partner to learn about their day and, most important, to work out a conflict before it becomes a war.

When this attention is lacking, nothing can get resolved. When conflicts are swept under the carpet, the space grows more contaminated, and the carpet can begin to look like the Swiss Alps—way too steep to climb. We either explode or withdraw, depending on how we deal with stress. Meanwhile, the chasm grows wider and morphs into an even bigger disconnect.

In that case, says Schleifer, a conflict can become an opportunity!

What does she mean? It's a chance for growth, change, and raising the level of intimacy. Conflict, when handled with care, can drain the relational swamp, clear the air, and cleanse the polluted space, but only if we know how to do it, apply it, and integrate it into our daily lives, just as one brushes their teeth and showers each day.

This is when our survival suit disappears, and our essence emerges.

Here's how it works: A couple sits in two chairs, facing one another, leaning slightly forward, about eighteen inches apart (forty-five centimeters for metric lovers), with both feet on the floor. Why eighteen inches? In neurobiology, that is the distance needed for presencing. Think about holding a baby in your arms. There would be approximately eighteen inches between the baby and you. That's the kind of intimate space we need to make this work.

I then instruct the woman to place her legs inside her partners and to just breathe. I encourage them to focus on their partner with warm eyes and an open heart. After all, the assumption is they both showed up and hired me to be their change agent, so resistance is not exactly welcome.

"Look into the eyes of your partner. Be grateful that you are alive. Feel your aliveness as you continue to breathe and see who showed up!"

I point from one to the other.

"Look who's here with you!"

This is when I give them a moment to "see" each other.

"Notice the landscape of your partner's face, and without saying a word, thank your partner for being here. Place your palms together, holding hands slightly apart on your laps, and breathe deeply. Take a few moments to feel the skin of your partner in a touch only the two of you know. Remember, the skin is our largest organ. Feel the inside of the palm of your partner, touch their fingers, and take another deep breath. Allow yourself to see the child in your partner's eyes. Imagine how they might have looked as children. Stay focused on each other's eyes, which are the true windows of the soul. Stay still and silent and breathe again."

All the while, I keep shifting my index finger back and forth from one pair of eyes to the other, as a reminder to stay focused.

This dual meditation should take about five minutes, and it should feel like a dance. That is the art of presencing, of being present with your partner. I'm sure that couples who want to reconnect can afford five minutes a day to nourish their relationship. What about you?

In his book, *The Road Less Traveled*, M. Scott Peck, MD, defines love as "the willingness to extend yourself to nurture another person's spiritual growth as well as your own."

I have never known a better definition. Words are not important when two partners remain present. What we know from neurobiology is that the brain is the only organ in the body that cannot self-regulate. It needs another brain. When two brains resonate together, the central nervous system calms down. This creates a brain bridge.

Barbra Streisand's song, "People Who Need People," says it all. It does not imply codependency at all. Instead, it means that for people to stay connected, they need each other. Our brains crave connection and attachment. It fills the heart with a sense of belonging and makes a person feel that they matter. It confirms our existence in this world! Isn't that what each of us needs? Isn't that what couples want and need in a relationship?

We all want to feel as if we belong—to those we love and the world. We want to feel loved and lovable—and to experience a secure attachment to another human being, something we may never have experienced throughout our lives. Lacking these human needs creates chaos, low self-esteem, and a collage of negative feelings about oneself and others, which result in depression and alienation. Eventually, this makes its way into the cells of our body and affects our immune system in potentially damaging ways. It can also disturb the synchronicity of our mind-body connection, leaving us emotionally starved and full of relentless stress, which can often cause disease.

Presencing is not a difficult process to learn if you want to enrich and restore the love you once had or the love you wish to maintain. That's because love is like a living organism. It needs to be fed and nurtured, protected and secured. It requires attention, not unlike a plant that needs sunlight, water, fertilizer, and the correct environment. Given what it needs, a plant will flourish. Many of us as children did not have our needs met. We lacked proper nourishment, even if our plates were full at dinnertime. Consequently, we keep searching for this kind of love in our partners, often repeating the past and eventually giving up, thinking we picked the wrong partner when, in fact, we are just trying to get it right.

When your partner receives what they need, your relationship will benefit. It's simple, but it takes time, commitment, and money, which is worth the investment!

Celebrating the Experts

Harville Hendrix, PhD, created a style of couple's therapy that focuses on relational counseling, transforming a conflict into an opportunity to grow and heal. Schleifer adapted her work to create the potential for the same outcome. Each contributed to helping couples reconnect.

There have been endless contributions made in the field of couple counseling. New and improved techniques are emerging all the time. There is no one way or best way. This is determined by what works best for each therapist and what clicks with the couples. Many therapists, like me, incorporate several modalities to apply as needed. It's like golf. If you only have one club in your golf bag, chances are you will play a less-than-satisfying game of golf. When techniques are synthesized to produce a desired outcome, it often generates a new technology. Many therapists, including me, have stacked, compiled, modified, and included many of the modalities used by wizard-like therapists, adding original insights and ideas.

I have employed the techniques of several, some of whom I've already mentioned, including the works of John Bradshaw, *The New York Times* bestselling author and creator of Creating Healthy Relationships, which uses his fair fighting rules, inner child work, and work within the recovering community, as well as how to employ the Change model for more effective communication. I have studied with Lori and Morris Gordon, who developed PAIRS. I have utilized the works of NLP (neuro-linguistics programming) and had the privilege of studying with Richard Bandler and John Grinder, who deliberated in detail the works of Virginia Satir (family therapy) and Milton Erickson, MD, (hypnosis), with the purpose of using teachings from those that do it best in the fields of sales, education, and therapy. I attended workshops and listened to the tapes of Tony Robbins and viewed recordings of Esther Perel and John Gottman, who introduced the concept of *The Four Horsemen of the Apocalypse*, a metaphor that describes the four main behaviors that will cause decimation of a relationship. I am certified as a master technician in EMDR (eye movement desensitization and reprocessing), having had the honor of studying with Francine Shapiro, who discovered this amazing technology to resolve PTSD. PTSD plays an important role in relationships, when one person (or both) unconsciously brings their past into the present, disrupting and polluting the relational space and causing chaos and doom.

This has been my life's work, and I have learned that any technique only works as well as the person using it. What's most important is giving every couple the feeling that they matter . . . because they do!

The Challenge of Letting Go

Learning to play the piano begins with practicing scales. Driving a car requires a license, which can only be secured after sufficient instruction. Learning a sport demands tedious repetition, as does voice training and anything worth learning. It does not always come naturally, even if an instinctive talent is present. Learning any new performance or activity needs instruction, preparation, and cultivation.

The art of presencing also needs to be learned. It is something we do naturally as children when we discover the world with wonder and curiosity. It is only when we grow into adulthood and our survival suit is glued on to our bodies that we forget what we once knew so well. Beginning again is like learning how to play an instrument correctly after stumbling through it on our own. It can feel contrived and staged, as do all new acquired behaviors. Once this is accomplished, the results are well worth the effort and extremely gratifying.

When we learn how to be present with our partners, three invisible connectors can be introduced. However, they cannot be successful without presencing. This is our entry into the first invisible connector, the relational space, which opens the door to crossing the bridge and finally approaching the encounter.

Now that we understand the art of presencing, let's consider its effect in the relational space where a couple resides, just as children share relational space on a playground and where pets feel at home. This space automatically becomes contaminated if a couple does not know how to take care of it.

Presencing is the starting point of making any space clean. When couples look into each other's warm eyes and sense an open heart, something magical can happen. The central nervous system relaxes. Tension in the body is reduced. Shoulders that might be tight go soft. Blood pressure drops. Tears may well up. This may be the first time two people have looked deeply and lovingly into each other's eyes.

"Oh! It's you!" Schleifer often bellows, demonstrating the start of presencing.

Couples usually smile. I ask them to thank the other for showing up and being present. The space is now fertile for crossing the bridge. I give specific instructions on how to do this. One partner assumes the role of the host, while the other is the visitor. Each person must choose their own role. Sometimes, this produces a conflict.

"Choose the role that would best benefit your relationship," I tell them.

There is usually a pregnant pause before one party responds.

"Okay, I'll be the host or visitor," says one party, leaving the other satisfied with the opposite role.

Most couples feel awkward starting the process. They don't know how to be present or what to say, so it is necessary to coach them and teach them to let go.

Anne and David

This couple came into my office perplexed, anxious, and deeply hurt. They had been carrying a gunny sack of anger and emotional pain for many years. Divorce seemed to be their next step. A relative had told them about ECCT (encounter-centered couples therapy) and referred them to me for counseling. Reluctantly, Anne made the appointment, and both showed up early on a Monday morning. Anne immediately spoke.

"This is our last resort. We are tired of fighting and have no more resources. We have both been in therapy, individually and as a couple. Nothing seemed to work. Our decision was to separate and then file for divorce. David's sister insisted that we make an appointment with you. He said we could always get a divorce. Give it this last chance, so here we are."

David shrugged and nervously responded, "Yep. That's right.

Too much time, too much pain, and not enough to rebuild. I was not looking forward to this visit, but we both decided not to throw in the towel, at least not yet. I guess we both want it to work but are exhausted trying with no results. My sister saw you with her husband a few years back and said you saved their marriage. They told us they still use the tools you taught them and feel grateful to you for the work you did with them."

"Quite honestly, I did not save their marriage. They did. I gave them the resources they needed and instilled hope. They took the tools home, practiced, and made it a priority, or it would not have been successful."

The pain I saw with Anne and David was palpable. But beneath the obvious current of despair was a glimmer of hope. That is how our session began. After acquiring some history, I learned that they had been married for eighteen years, had two children, a son, Timothy, fifteen, and a daughter, Belinda, who had just turned thirteen. I asked if they had any pets. They shared that Daisy, a cocker spaniel rescue, had been with them nearly eight years.

"Do you have a photo of your children and Daisy?"

David took out his wallet, which contained photos of the children and Daisy. Anne's phone displayed recent photos of the family. Daisy was in the front row.

I smiled.

"You are lucky. You have a beautiful family."

As they both agreed, Anne welled up with tears.

"Yes, we do," she said. "That's one reason we're here."

We took a moment of silence to reflect on Anne's words. Then, I asked them to demonstrate how they worked on conflict.

"Take any issue that becomes an argument and show me how it sounds and looks."

I sat next to them as they squirmed on the sofa, bewildered at how to respond.

"I'm not sure what you mean," David said.

"Just show me how you discuss a conflict."

"You mean choose something we fight about?"

"Exactly. Choose an issue and pretend I'm a fly on the wall and let me see how you communicate. You have thirteen minutes to create this scenario so I can observe you. Then, I will call *stop*, and you will do so even if you are in the middle of a sentence."

They looked confused. They each wanted me to know that this was something neither of them were ever asked to do in any of their previous therapy sessions. I told them I understood, that there was a method to this madness, and to just be patient. They chose a common conflict. David chose how Anne mismanages money. It could have been any topic. I was interested in their means of communication, just as a physician examines an X-ray.

It took less than a minute before their emotions flared up and their voices rose, quickly morphing into a vitriolic shouting match. Their body language reflected their tone and dialectical exchange. Arms waved, legs shook, and bodies shifted, either moving toward or away from each other. As they continued shouting, their faces became more and more flushed, and they seemed unaware I was in the room. Their dialogue took on a life of its own.

At precisely thirteen minutes, I stopped them. They looked at each other, then turned to me. Anne took a deep breath.

"Whew. I'm exhausted."

David nodded.

"Me too. We do this too often, and it leads to nothing but frustration and futility. I can't keep this up. My blood pressure rises, and I need a drink to calm me down. It doesn't work."

"I imagine this is your style of dealing with conflict," I said. "Right?"

"Yep! This is us in action. But why thirteen minutes?"

"That's all the time needed to observe the process. Imagine if someone was in your home and heard you both as you are and suddenly shouted 'stop' when things were becoming out of control. Everyone present, including Daisy, would be greatly relieved."

This is when the teaching began.

"You were the Wigerian couple."

They looked at me as if I were speaking a foreign language. Wigerian is the title that had been given to my colleagues and me when we attended a master class presented by Schleifer as we began our training in ECCT. The Wigerian couple is a fictitious word that metaphorically means the couple that comes from another planet. They only speak Wigerian.

"I want you to imagine you were just in a diner and saw another couple sitting across from you. That couple represents who you were a few minutes ago. You were able to see them, but because they were from Wigeria, you could not understand a word they spoke. Tell me your observations, based solely on what you saw. Remember that you could not understand them, as they spoke a language you've never heard. Describe what you noticed and interpreted, and then tell me why."

This was not easy. They had difficulty keeping what they heard, rather than what they saw, out of the content. I had to pause them a few times until they understood.

"She was very distraught," said Anne.

"Give me evidence without any words she might have said."

"Well, she raised her voice. Her demeanor changed rapidly. She went from calm to anger in a matter of moments after her partner attacked her."

"How do you know he attacked her?"

"That was easy. He began insulting her."

"How do you know they were insults, Annie? You don't know their language."

"She appeared angry after he spoke. I imagine he said something she didn't like."

"Of course he did," said David.

"How do you know?" I said. "You also don't understand the language."

"Because that's exactly what I did just before Annie blew up."

This went on for about twenty minutes. The purpose was to objectify their behavior so they could see how they looked if they were observing themselves, which most couples can't do. When the process was complete and they understood the value of the exercise, they could see themselves in a mirror, becoming aware of how this behavior impacted their relationship.

"Oh, my god!" both said simultaneously.

"Oh, my god is right! Imagine how this affects your kids and Daisy if they are chronically subjected to this behavior. Imagine how this destroys love, affection, sex, and the relationship."

I said this without judgment or criticism, as it's basically a scientific fact of what can happen when two adults poison a home for its other inhabitants.

"This is what John Gottman refers to as *The Four Horsemen of the Apocalypse*: contempt, criticism, judgment, and stonewalling. They destroy relationships."

Annie and David looked at each other with sorrow and shame. They described their space as sad, scary, shameful, pathetic, and sick, before adding the word *insightful*. I repeated each word after it had been spoken. Those were the words they reflected to me when I asked them to describe the space between them after the work was done.

Now they were ready to learn the art of presencing. I moved two chairs to face each other and invited them to sit. The teaching and instruction of presencing was done, and they sat quietly, reflecting on their shared experience. I told them what to do and how to do it, and they followed my instructions. Tears flowed as I stayed with them, reminding them to stay connected through locking their eyes on each other. No words were spoken, and no questions were asked. I heard their sniffles, sobs, and breathing as I facilitated this dynamic process of transformation. I felt privileged and blessed to be their change agent.

At that moment, I knew that this couple would escape the prison they had cocreated. As they sat in the eye of this beautiful storm, I felt so lucky to be their benign witness.

What Do We Do Now?

The art of being present is not only the preparation for crossing the bridge and embracing what needs to be encountered. It is also a gateway to learning how to listen with a third ear. This concept was introduced by psychoanalyst Theodor Reik, and it refers to the practice of listening for the deeper layers of meaning so we can glean what has not been said outright. It means perceiving the emotional underpinnings conveyed when someone is speaking to you. Most importantly, it teaches us how to be conscious, patient, and attentive to another person, which is lacking in most relationships. This type of active listening is the key to ensuring respect for each other. It offers anyone hope for repairing or reigniting the love that is the foundation of all relationships.

*Out of suffering have emerged
the strongest souls;
the most massive characters
are seared with scars.*

—KAHLIL GIBRAN

Chapter Six

No More Judgment, No More Criticism, No More Blame, No More BS

IN THE PREVIOUS CHAPTER, I described the importance of presencing. If your partner doesn't understand the value of being present or care enough to learn how, conflict will never be resolved.

Being present means staying focused and mindful of the other person. This is accomplished by looking into the eyes of your partner and staying conscious in the here and now. You may know this as "living in the moment."

This is the precursor to crossing the bridge, the next invisible connector.

In *The Kaminsky Method*, a television series on Netflix, Michael Douglas plays the owner and acting coach of his school. In one episode, he teaches the art of mirroring, an elementary acting exercise for beginners.

Mirroring might as well be called presencing, as its goal is to teach students how to stay present, fully engaged, and in the moment with their partner. The goal is identical in presencing. Douglas has his students mirror or replicate exactly what their partner is doing, as if there were a mirror between them. If their partner's hand creates a circle, their hand follows along, emulating the exact behavior.

This is precisely what is done in crossing the bridge.

With so many distractions in the day, this is not easy, but it's necessary to achieve effective communication. Once presencing is learned—and I say learned because being present does not come naturally—a couple can move forward to conscious, active listening, understanding, and resolution. In most families, our role models are our parents, who did not always exemplify this essential trait in communication. Therefore, in our own defense, how were we to know how to be present? We only know what we know!

The Curse of the Pot Roast

My mother was not the best cook. It wasn't her fault, as she learned how to cook from her mother, my grandmother. Grandma Eva came from Poland to America at the turn of the twentieth century to join my grandfather, Moishe, who fled Warsaw to escape the persecution of Jews and serve in the military. Like most immigrants, Eva arrived with little, but she managed to bring a small tin pan that her mother had given her before she left Poland, along with a few other salient items. My grandmother used it to cook everything she had learned from her mother. Being impoverished, not unlike Golda and Tevya from *Fiddler on the Roof*, they cooked with bare essentials, including inexpensive cuts of kosher meat, and condiments were always scarce.

I never knew about Heinz ketchup until I was in my twenties. My mother went to the Thrifty Market in South Beach, where many poor, first-generation Jews migrated and bought only nonbrand items. She, like her mother, was a champion shopper. My father used to say that she could take a dollar and turn it into four. He also said I could take four dollars and turn it into one!

That pan was a household item until my mother gave it to me when I married. I kept it, primarily for sentimental reasons, until I was nearly fifty years old.

My mother used that pan to make pot roast, otherwise known as brisket. I hated it. We had it every Thursday, so when I got off the bus from school and neared our apartment, I could already smell the unsavory, odious flavor of our inevitable dinner.

"Shit, it's Thursday. Pot roast."

My mother went to the kosher butcher and bought the cheapest piece of meat, which was known as brashstekle. It was tough, first because it was kosher and not aged, and second because it was the cheapest cut of meat from the bottom of the cow's belly. No one knew its origin. They only knew that it was affordable. No one in my family has ever been to a restaurant and ordered pot roast or tasted anyone else's pot roast, so they had no frame of reference to judge their own cooking, and for them, it was tasty.

My mother took the meat, laid it fat-side-up in the tin pan, and folded over the ends because the pan was too small. She added a potato, an onion, a couple carrots, salt, pepper, and a bottle of Thrifty Maid ketchup. Somehow, we swallowed it, probably out of obligation.

"Why don't you get a bigger pan?" I always asked her.

"It makes juice when you fold it over!"

In Yiddish, this response is referred to as a Bubba Miseh—an old wives' tale—which some of us simply call bullshit.

But I accepted her explanation. It made sense to me as a teenager, and that was how I learned to make pot roast. When I became a young bride, I acquired a cookbook created by a group of women in my neighborhood, all of whom were members of a local affiliate of a national cancer organization. We all shared recipes from our personal history. This is how I learned how to make brisket. For some reason, pot roast was not included in our makeshift cookbook, and I wasn't about to offer my mother's version. However, I used my mother's tin pan that she gave me when I married, so the meat had its original home for roasting. Unlike my mother, though, I followed the brisket recipe that became my children's favorite meal, even until today.

While married to my last husband, Mike, a meat fabricator and proprietor of a gourmet grocery business in Miami Beach, similar to Dean & Deluca in New York City, he asked if I could make pot roast.

"Pot roast! You like pot roast?"

"Yes, pot roast. I love pot roast!"

I recalled making a face, screwing up my eyes, and wondering how anyone could like pot roast. Just the sound of those two words triggered my olfactory senses and resurrected the abhorrent smell that had been dormant in my brain for quite some time.

"Why don't you just bring it home from the hot counter in the store? Or better yet, just bring it home from the freezer, and I will heat it up."

Mike looked at me, shaking his head.

"No!" he said. "I would prefer you make it at home."

It is important to note that his mother was an amazing cook. In fact, she founded the grocery store in the 1940s, preparing recipes she had created and brought with her from back home in Lithuania. I didn't know what to say, as I realized I had no excuse that would be acceptable, so I capitulated to his wishes and went to a kosher butcher, a place I had never visited in my adult life.

"May I have a piece of brashstekle, please?"

"Brashstekle! What are you going to use it for?"

The butcher sounded strangely curious.

"Pot roast."

"That's not the best piece of meat for a nice pot roast. It's used mainly for soup flavoring."

I appreciated his advice but chose the cut of meat that my mother always used, never considering that he might know better than my mother. When it came to cooking, I was still in the same trance that I had been in since birth.

I went home, took out the meat, and laid it exactly as my mother had always done in the pan. I folded the ends over, adding the same ingredients she had always used, except I used a different brand of ketchup. I chose Heinz, an upgrade in my mind, and a bit of garlic, which was my own touch. It wasn't long before I heard Mike open the door to our apartment.

"What stinks?"

I thought it was strange that he had the same response I had when I was a teenager, coming home on Thursdays to the same putrid smell.

"It's the pot roast you asked me to make. It will be ready in a few minutes."

Mike opened the oven. "Joni, the pot's too small. Look, the meat doesn't even fit in the pan."

"This is the pan my mother used. You have to fold the meat over to make the gravy."

It should come as no surprise that our dinner was tossed in the garbage. Mike asked me never to buy that cut of meat again. He was happy to share his mother's recipe, which did not include kosher meat and was not aged or tenderized. I was greatly relieved, as I knew her recipe was a hard act to follow. The following day, he brought home the pot roast from the hot counter. The smell was nothing like what I remembered. Dinner was delicious, and I loved it!

Who Knew?

It's not that I didn't have a dozen or more cookbooks on my kitchen shelf. It's not that I couldn't Google a recipe on my own. I just did what came naturally. I made the pot roast as I had learned it from my mother, the same way I learned how to communicate. My parents never resolved anything. Their differences were settled with either my mother capitulating to my father or my father having a personal protest and giving everyone in the household "silent violence," which meant he stonewalled us. Most of the time, any conflict was swept under the carpet until the carpet began to resemble the terrain of the Swiss Alps. After a few days, all was forgotten—until the next blowup.

This story of the stinky pot roast shows how we only know what we know. We inherit what we were exposed to as children and repeat it in our adult relationships, believing this is how it should be!

When we don't know how to be present, it becomes a multigenerational tradition, like the pan my grandmother gave my mother, which my mother handed down to me. We assume that is the way it should happen. It becomes a legacy learned from our family of origin. Even though we may think so at first, doing what comes naturally doesn't necessarily mean that it's right, healthy, or makes sense.

The analogy of my mother's pot roast generalizes how we carry forth family systems and traditions when we marry and create our own families. Many of our behaviors, thoughts, beliefs, and values come from how we were raised and how our parents were raised. These patterns go back generations, and it's only when they don't work with our new partners that conflict begins.

As Schleifer says with great enthusiasm, "Conflict is a friend. What an opportunity!"

A Model for Change

Couples can only grow when they can resolve conflict, which ultimately raises their levels of intimacy. But this can only happen with the art of presencing!

In his work with couples, John Gottman describes what he

refers to as "The Four Horsemen of the Apocalypse": criticism, contempt, defensiveness, and stonewalling. In the New Testament, the Four Horsemen of the Apocalypse is a metaphor depicting the end of times, which Gottman borrows to depict the demise of a relationship. These four behaviors will destroy any relationship if they become a chronic characteristic of a couple's communication style.

In the Change Model, John Bradshaw states that criticism can be replaced with a complaint or a concern, as did Lori and Morris Gordon, the founders of PAIRS.

"You" messages are replaced with "I" messages. "I" messages are self-responsible statements representing what one sees or hears—how one feels—to go along with how one interprets and what one needs. After expressing these concerns, a contract is made.

Individual parts of the model include perception (what is seen or heard), feelings, thoughts (what is interpreted), and what a person needs. Finally, after genuine communication, a verbal contract secures an agreement.

For example, consider the following dialogue: "When I saw you spending so much time with Mary at the party last night, I felt hurt and upset. I imagined that you were flirting with her, and I needed your attention to be on me. Can we agree that the next time we are in a mixed social situation, you are conscious of spending less time with other women and more time with me?"

This recipe for open communication essentially eliminates the word "you" and reduces the instinct for being defensive and the probability of an argument. Challenging your partner with the word "you" instead of "I" is an invitation to a fight. Your partner will become defensive, ready to argue that it was not the case. The space immediately becomes dangerous, and you both alternatively react to the danger in the space.

According to Schleifer, in a situation like this, two types of people begin to behave accordingly. Hailstormers become more aggressive, usually raising their voices, while turtles become withdrawn and shut down. Neither party feels honored or heard, and the fighting escalates from there. Make no mistake. Hailstormers and turtles can be of either gender. Men and women don't have exclusive rights to these behaviors.

In addition to refraining from using the "you" word, such as "You are always late. I know you will never be on time," avoid using words like always, never, should, and must. They express a demand and are not helpful in a dialogue.

Crossing the Bridge

Let's examine the second invisible connector, eliminating criticism, defensiveness, contempt, or stonewalling. In *crossing the bridge*, there is no dialogue between partners—only a visit and an encounter. It creates all the elements needed for a healthy, conscious relationship by providing a platform for each partner to consider and understand their partner's perceptions, feelings, interpretations, needs, and wishes. Its economy of words, reflective listening, eye contact, and positive intention create a wavelength for growth, which deepens and intensifies the relational space between partners.

What was formerly polluted becomes clean. What was previously fueling friction and upheaval morphs into understanding and empathy. Once this technique is learned and practiced, conflict becomes an opportunity for growth, closeness, and connection.

So how does it work? Let's observe a couple who came to me for help.

Anne and David

Remember these two from the previous chapter? A week later, Anne and David arrived at my office for their follow-up appointment. They brought a framed professional photograph of their children and placed it on a table in front of them. I had placed fresh flowers there to create a warm and inviting atmosphere. I already had two chairs in position, facing each other. Anne and David took the cue and sat in the chairs without my instruction. They told me that the week since our meeting had been better, which I was delighted to hear. I congratulated them once more for making the effort to try again.

"That was a remarkable exercise you had us do," said Anne. "I didn't realize how emotionally drained I was just from watching us in the diner."

David agreed. They could reflect on their behavior as they recognized their emotional fatigue and failure to solve their issue. By objectifying themselves in the diner, they clearly saw how their communication style was damaging and futile. They were also reminded about how their behavior affects their children.

"So once again," I said. "Do I have a big fat 'yes' from both of you?"

They looked at each other and glanced back at me. Anne nodded, followed by a nod and a shrug from David.

"That is not terribly big or fat. I need to be certain of your intention. Let's try it again. Do I have a big fat 'yes' from both of you?"

Both responded simultaneously, as if I had commanded them, "Yes!"

They looked at each other again and then turned their attention to me. I told them that we would not be successful without a strong commitment. "Let's get started. Position yourselves as I had instructed you last week."

Anne and David sat eighteen inches apart, eyeball to eyeball. They leaned forward, placed their hands in each other's, and looked into each other's eyes. The emotional fatigue, so apparent last week, was gone, and they appeared eager to begin.

"Lean forward and connect so that your eyes never leave each other. Place your hands together and feel the familiar touch of each other. Thank your partner for showing up, but just with your eyes! Now, still without words, share your hopes, wishes, and dreams with each other. Look deeply into your partner's eyes and let them know how grateful you are to be alive and for all the things you share together. You can do this with your eyes. Words are not necessary." Since my chair was in the middle, apart about a foot from theirs, I continued moving my finger slowly back and forth between their eyes as a reminder for them to stay connected to each other.

"This is how you discover the landscape in your partner's face. When we begin crossing the bridge, you will learn a new language. Just stay with each other."

When I asked them in a soft voice to see the child in the other, as if their partner were seven years old, tears welled up in both their eyes.

"Stay together. Just keep looking, with an open heart and soft eyes. You can do this. Just stay focused and remain connected."

The process lasted about five or six minutes. The next step was to ask Anne and David to share how the space felt between them after they did the presencing. They were aware of the shift in the space and responded with words that seemed to surprise them.

"It feels warm," Anne said.

"Safe," said David.

I asked them to toss out words that described the space. This part of the process was slow to unfold. I repeated each word they shared. By reflecting back on their words, Anne and David were able to learn what active listening is all about.

We moved next into the three wildest dreams.

I had them write down three dreams they wanted to actualize in their lifetime. The dreams were called *wild*, so they could imagine whatever they wanted to put on their respective horizon without boundaries. When I asked them to share their dreams, they were surprised to learn that they were identical. As Anne and David read aloud, I wrote down all three shared dreams. I read it back to them so they could hear their dreams spoken, which became another reflective listening lesson unwittingly planted into their subconscious brains.

Anne and David were ready to cross the bridge to the world of the other.

I gave them explicit instructions to prepare them for the visit and the encounter, which make up the third invisible connector. I asked them to leave behind their perceptions, stories, prejudices, emotions, beliefs, preconceived notions, and behaviors. All of those had to stay back on their side of the bridge. They could only take a plastic bag with a passport and visa. It had to be plastic so they could see it was only those items. Everything else had to be left on their side of the bridge. Otherwise, it would be considered "an illegal import." I would act as a customs officer to ensure that their "stuff" would remain in their world and not be illegally transported to their partner's world.

Next, Anne and David had to choose who would be the visitor and who would be the host. They were both reluctant, but after intrapersonal consideration, Anne chose to be the host, and David was content to be the visitor.

I took my time to coach them through this process, explaining their respective roles in detail. They understood the concept, but both acknowledged their anxiety. David's leg shook rapidly. Anne sat quietly, holding back tears. I decided to slow the process down by doing a breathing meditation to help them relax. As they began focusing on their breath, I noticed David's leg stopped shaking and Anne released her tears.

"I'm scared," Anne said. "What if I can't do this? What if I get it wrong?"

"There's no right or wrong," I said. "Everything that will

happen has a positive intention. We'll go slowly, and I will help you every step of the way."

Once they understood the rules and goals, we began. I pulled my chair closer and leaned over so I could assist them gently as we moved into the ritual.

"Anne, as the host, you will invite David to cross the bridge and come over to your neighborhood. Then you are going to take him down a street called... whatever name you want to give it, anything you want to share with David. For example, it can be called the street of misunderstanding, the street of fear, anxiety, loneliness, or worry—whatever you want to name it. So, it will sound like this: 'David, I would like to invite you to my neighborhood, down my street called *fill in the blank*.' Do you understand?"

Anne nodded and waited for me to continue. I kept reminding them to look into each other's eyes and stay connected through every beat of the process.

"It's not easy to stay present, but it's absolutely necessary. This encounter is a meeting of your human essences, your two souls, and your two life forces. It allows you to drop your survival suits, the protective armor you may not even realize you've been wearing for so long, so that your authentic selves can emerge—perhaps for the first time. From now on, you will not need them because they do not serve any positive purpose. You will soon discover that beneath the suits you have been wearing for so long is the real you."

I spoke softly to David, giving him instructions on his role as the visitor.

"After Anne invites you to visit her neighborhood and the street she has chosen and named, you will respond as if you have been invited to visit someone's home. You'll say, 'Thank you, Anne, for the invitation,' and then repeat what she requested, with something like 'I am happy to cross the bridge to your neighborhood and visit the street called *fill in the blank*.'"

I told them there was an imaginary bridge between their neighborhoods. In neurobiology, this bridge is called the brain bridge. Our brain is the only organ in the body that cannot self-regulate. It can only do that through the resonance of another brain when new neural pathways are created with the capacity to become more relationally intelligent. The brain's plasticity makes it capable of changing old habits and creating new ones in the service of oneself and the relationship.

When you hear someone say, "This is who I am. I have always been like this. I cannot change. Just accept me as I am," you should know that it is not true. We can change because of the flexible plasticity in our brains. We only have to choose to make the changes and learn how to manifest them. We can grow further if and when we choose to do so. This teaching reflects information well-known to psychologists, psychiatrists, and other mental health professionals.

David was instructed to slowly walk across the imaginary bridge and arrive in Anne's neighborhood. Once there, he would announce his presence. Anne would thank him for coming, and the encounter would begin. After prepping each regarding their roles, I instructed the host to speak with as few words as possible, using not more than five or six.

Anne paused for a long time. "I don't know what to say."

"Say the name of your street, for starters."

Anne hesitated and rolled her eyes upward, as if picturing what her street represented and what she wanted to call it. After a few silent moments, she said, "I want to invite you down the street of not feeling safe."

David followed my instructions perfectly.

"Anne, what I heard you say is that you want to invite me to your neighborhood to visit the street called 'not feeling safe.' Am I with you?"

I gave David a nod of approval and leaned into him once more, smiling, as I told him what his response should be: "Tell me more."

David responded. "Tell me more."

Silence.

No one moved.

Finally, Anne looked at me as if to ask me what comes next. I spoke briefly, telling her to describe her street in five words or less.

"I'm scared to express my feelings to you," she said to David.

That was more than five words, but it was specific, sensory-based information, so it was acceptable.

David looked perplexed.

"You have nothing to be afraid of," he said.

I stopped the process to explain that in this ritual of crossing the bridge, there is no dialogue. David was only to repeat Anne's words and respond with one of two phrases: "Am I with you?" and "Tell me more."

"You mean I can't respond to her?" he said. "I can't have thoughts about what she says?"

He was visibly annoyed. "Then when can I have my turn to respond?" he said.

I had to reinforce the purpose of this encounter and review the rules so that David could understand that this was not intended to be a dialogue. This took some time, but he eventually understood, and we began again.

Anne's responses deepened as David began to use the allowed phrases appropriately. She began to feel safe and shared her feelings. David remained patient. Instead of talking over her, as he had done in the past, he listened, and the look on his face gave Anne the impression that he was hearing her and repeating the words she said.

There was no shouting, stonewalling, criticism, contempt, or defensiveness—just listening and repeating her words. He only rolled his eyes once—a real no-no—so I alerted him that rolling your eyes is an illegal import, which comes from his neighborhood on the other side of the bridge. I asked him to take it back from where it came. They shared some laughter, which gave levity to the process.

Making David conscious of his behavior and explaining the destructive effect it had on his relationship with Anne made him more mindful. He said he would try to refrain from doing it again.

"We don't expect perfection," I said, "only progress. This is not a one-time event! It's a process! It takes time, commitment, and a whole lot of patience and practice. It is a new way of communicating, and you'll soon see that the results are worthwhile."

Several times during this first encounter in my office, David's responses did not exactly mirror the words Anne had spoken. Whenever that occurred, I instructed Anne to say, "You got most of it. Here's what I want you to hear and understand." David tried again until Anne felt as if he was genuinely with her and that her words and needs were resonating with him. This openness and attention to detail are necessary to ensure a complete connection.

Occasionally, both partners made illegal imports. Each time one slipped in, I paused the process and explained it again until they got it. It took the entire two hours for them to cross the bridge one time. This is why I like to have a couple with me for two days; it allows the process to be fluid and unfold at a pace that suits their particular personalities and relationship.

It took Anne another half an hour and quite a few tears before she felt a sense of completion, that she had no more to say. Throughout the process, David tried hard not to respond. He sat quietly, as I had taught him, and waited for any waves of emotion to quiet down before he would once again say to Anne, "Tell me more." I reminded David that she needed time to express her feelings and that he needed to give her permission to take that time. Whenever a wave of emotion surged, they allowed it to complete its energy before continuing. I reminded Anne that she had to provide the same benefit for David when it was his turn.

This was a lesson in empathy and compassion, which had been lacking in their daily communication.

During our time together, new neural pathways began forming in their brains. Anne recognized that David did have the capacity to listen, and David recognized that Anne was entitled to her feelings. Each time Anne spoke with a few words, and David repeated them, adding the phrases we had rehearsed, the give-and-take became easier. They began to integrate the process and could hear one another and stay present. I ensured they maintained eye contact, which emphasizes that the heartbeat of the exchanges is authentic and loving.

What Do We Do Now?

After the visit, I asked David to summarize what he had learned from his visit to Anne's neighborhood. As she listened to him, Anne felt genuinely heard and understood, relieved and relaxed. Next, I had Anne and David offer each other three "appreciations," followed by sharing what was most important to them. Then I had them write down five things they learned, which they shared aloud. Finally, I asked them to describe the space, using only one word at a time. With each word expressed, I repeated it back, reinforcing the art and craft of effective listening.

When our time was up, I asked if they would be interested in spending two full days with me, explaining how this would be even more beneficial. They were open to the idea and said they would consider it and let me know. I told them to practice what we had done in the session, giving them a tip sheet with the steps, including putting two chairs together and facing each other in a room when they would not be disturbed, such as when their children were asleep.

I was not surprised when Anne and David called me during the week, telling me they had decided to commit to the two-day intensive. We were all excited to make an appointment two weeks in advance, leaving all of us time to clear our schedules and prepare.

The next chapter reveals what happened.

> *"A bird may love a fish but where would they build a home together?"*
>
> —TEVYE, FROM *FIDDLER ON THE ROOF*, BY JOSEPH STEIN

Chapter Seven

Swimming to Paradise: A Bridge Over Troubled Waters

AS YOU WITNESSED in the previous chapter, David successfully completed their first bridge crossing. Due to time restrictions, I was limited in expanding the process to the next level, which would have explored the etiology of one of Anne's most telling comments. When she said that she felt "unsafe to express her feelings," I wish we could have discovered more about where that came from and what continues to trigger these feelings.

Here's what we already know about human behavior: when we have a strong feeling about another person's behavior, it usually applies to the person who feels threatened in some way because of his or her history and not because of the person who triggered their response. Anne's reaction to David—feeling unsafe to express her feelings—was triggered by his communication style, but that was not the sole reason. It's more than likely that her reaction primarily stems from an earlier childhood experience. If there had been more time, I would have asked Anne to remember when it didn't feel safe to verbalize her feelings.

I would have told her to grab the first memory that came to her mind because a recollection from childhood would probably have emerged, allowing me to draw a line from the feeling she was having in my office back to a childhood trauma, which caused an early wound that could certainly still be reverberating today in her relationship with David. The story she would have shared and the feelings associated with her memory would have enlightened David and helped him better understand Anne's history. When this happens as part of the *crossing the bridge* process, empathy surfaces, and a new learning pattern is revealed for both parties.

A Primer on Empathy

Empathy is the capacity to understand or feel what another person is experiencing from within their frame of reference by placing oneself in another person's position. Human beings are wired to be empathic. It's in our DNA. It's just that our own filters and history too often obfuscate our ability to be empathic, so we become reactive instead of proactive.

This might explain why David immediately became defensive when he heard Anne express her sense of feeling unsafe. When David and Anne return for a two-day intensive, giving us time to complete the ritual, I will demonstrate how this works when David is the host.

We know from working with individuals and couples that most of what triggers strong feelings or reactions usually originate from something that might have been repressed during childhood. That's just how our brains work. When we hurt early in life, we tend to inoculate ourselves against any more suffering. So, when something similar occurs in the present, it fires up all the neurons in the brain that have been dormant. Repressed feelings can suddenly surface, and a wound that never healed can be ripped open once again, often without warning and in a decidedly awkward situation.

Whenever something like this occurs, empathy becomes crucial.

Anne and David Dive In

When they arrived at my office on a Friday morning, two weeks after our initial appointment, I had a positive feeling about what we were about to accomplish. They brought a photo of their children, as I had reminded them to do, and they immediately noticed another floral arrangement I had already placed on the table.

After some chatting, reviewing the past two weeks, we were ready to begin. Anne and David revealed that they had practiced the bridge crossing several times, some successfully, and others not so much. They shared their frustrations and confusion, which I understood, and I told them their experience was normal.

"Nobody gets this perfect, especially after only one bridge crossing. It takes time, practice, patience, and perseverance. However, once you master the ritual, it becomes easier and integrated, much like brushing your teeth."

"Now it's my turn to be a host," said David, obviously eager to get started.

"Indeed, it is," I said. "Are you ready to cross the bridge?"

David and Anne sat in the same chairs I had set for them.

"Okay. Sit down and look at each other with a big open heart, soft eyes, and a generosity of spirit." I gave them a minute to get settled.

"Look who is here," I said with enthusiasm.

Schleifer had always welcomed her guests with a boisterous tone.

"Oh! It's you!" she would say, conveyed with a smile equal to her energetic voice. I did my best to provide a similar energy for Anne and David.

"Take a few breaths and show gratitude for each other's willingness to move the relationship forward. Thank each other with your eyes. Be grateful to be alive. Look at the photo of who is also in the room with us. Remember that this is not just for you.

It is for them as well. What your children learn from you will be carried into their future."

Anne and David responded right on cue. I reminded them of the roles of the visitor and the host. I reviewed the script, reminding David to use words sparingly, no more than five or six. Anne seemed a bit nervous, but both leaned forward as I had taught them and settled in quickly to their positions, eighteen inches apart.

David's opening words were purposeful and gentle.

"Anne, I would like to invite you to my neighborhood on a street called fear."

Anne took a few moments to respond.

"What I heard you say is that you want to invite me to your neighborhood on a street called fear. Am I with you?"

"Yes."

I nodded to Anne to respond with the words of the visitor.

"Tell me more."

"I'm scared when you disrespect our budget."

"What I heard you say is that you get scared when I disrespect our budget. Am I with you?"

"Yes. I feel you are not my partner."

"What I heard you say is that you feel that I am not your partner. Am I with you?"

"Yes.

Anne and David stayed focused on each other as these words passed between them. When they needed reminding, I used one finger to steer their eyes on each other. On several occasions, Anne did not respond exactly as David had spoken. Each time she did that, I had David repeat his words until Anne repeated them accurately and to his satisfaction. The object of this ritual is for one partner to learn the language of the other so that each can feel understood.

"When you don't stay within our budget, I get angry," David

said. "I feel as though you don't know the value of money."

"What I heard you say," said Anne, "is that when I don't stay within our budget, you get angry because you don't feel that I know the value of money. Am I with you?"

David nodded.

"Yes. It worries me because it puts a financial strain on me."

"What I heard you say is that it worries you because it creates a financial strain on you. Am I with you?"

The host and visitor continued on this path until David's fear actualized.

"I'm scared, Anne. I don't want us to be poor. You are going to drive us into the poor house."

This might seem contrived and staged, but it is neither. The purpose is to listen with every ounce of mindfulness the visitor can demonstrate so the host feels heard and understood. There is no dialogue or questions, only the words in the script I taught them to use. I stay with them, encouraging them to stay focused as I allow them to proceed without interruption. If they import something illegal from their own neighborhood, I stop the process and remind them to take it back. It is not an easy ritual, as the visitor is not always as mindful and present as we might prefer. However, when practiced and rehearsed, it can create new neural pathways that will elicit a connection, which both partners have been missing.

David Goes Deeper

David stayed with the process, not just with his words but through the heightened pitch of his feelings. As the ritual continued, his anger seemed to grow, and when it peaked, I felt compelled to step in to ask a question.

"When in your childhood were you afraid of being poor?"

As David sat silently, tears emerged, even though he tried to hold them back. One leg shook.

"We were poor when my mother left my father. They divorced when I was only a year old. I was scared that she would send me away because she didn't have money to take care of me. She told me this as soon as I had the ability to understand it."

The tears continued to pour out like an open faucet. "She told me she couldn't pay the bills and that I might have to live with my grandma." More tears. "She cried at night, and I didn't know what to say or do."

The child in David came out as he gave full expression to the fear he had held inside for so many years. In contrast, Anne came from a wealthy family, the daughter of a prominent banker and a mother who never had to work. Anne had no worries about not having enough to eat or being sent away. Her family enjoyed an abundance of riches, and she had everything she wanted growing up. Money, or the lack of it, was never in her lexicon.

Anne was frozen, tears rolling down her cheeks as she kept her eyes on David. She was now witnessing the child who still resided within the man she married. It was as if a new light suddenly went off in her mind. Anne always became angry whenever David confronted her about the things she bought for the house or their children. She never saw it as being spoiled or inconsiderate. In fact, from her perspective, Anne thought she was careful with money. David was adamant about not allowing her parents to subsidize any aspect of their life, so Anne had to learn to tighten her belt and be more conscious of what she spent.

Anne Sees David in a New Light

The ritual in my office presented a new paradigm shift for Anne. Watching David's essence emerge made her more empathic to his fear of being poor. Until now, she could never understand why he was so frugal or seemed so contemptuous. David was a good provider, earning more than six figures a year. They had an expensive home and were living comfortably.

Anne was not fully aware of David's early childhood trauma—until now. His story hit her like a bolt of lightning. Until this moment, she had always felt that David was demanding, unreasonable, and uncompromising. She would describe his behavior as "my way or the highway." She felt that he could be incorrigible and suspected that he might even have a borderline personality disorder.

Anne had never met the authentic David. He was always wearing his survival suit. Suddenly, after nine years of marriage, the real David revealed himself. Anne, who had never seen him cry or lose his tough composure, saw him as genuinely vulnerable. In these moments, she felt his pain, worry, and suffering.

The ritual was not over, however, as we continued into my favorite part. We needed a corrective experience for David, so I began to share what comes next.

"Anne, you will tell David a story as if he were a little boy. Tell him we live in the twenty-first century, where we have time machines. You are going to take David back to where he lived as a little boy, and you are going with him."

They both seemed perplexed but stayed with me.

"Where did you live when you were a little boy, David?"

"I lived here, in Miami."

"Do you remember your address?"

"Yes, I do. It was Twenty-Five Cedar Street."

"Oh, that's North Miami Beach or Aventura, right?"

"Yes, it is."

I knew the neighborhood. Even thirty years ago, it was an upper-middle-class part of the area. David's family could not have lived there if they were impoverished. When his mother was left on her own, with a child to raise, her fear-based language and tone about their finances made David feel insecure. Her words ran deep into his tender and unprotected brain. As an innocent and vulnerable child, he had no way of understanding their situation or the tools to see it from an adult perspective. David, like most children, absorbed the feelings of his primary parent, which left him feeling responsible for his imagined poverty. Even worse, he didn't have any resources to fix the problem. These primordial feelings stayed with him throughout his adult life and rose unexpectedly during his marriage. Anne was just being herself. She had no clue about David's terror. She always assumed he was a strong man, fully capable of earning a good living, basically fearless. Hearing his story was shocking to her.

"Okay, Anne. Are you ready to take David in the time machine back to visit his mother at Twenty-Five Cedar Street in North Miami Beach?"

"Yes, yes, I am. I will. Absolutely."

Anne had a sensitivity that David never realized she possessed. Throughout their marriage, they had both been living in their survival suits. Neither one of them ever really knew the other, not in the deepest ways this ritual can reveal. Now, in my office, Anne finally understood why David was always twisting his hair and shaking his foot.

"You are going to take David to the home where he once lived. When you land there and park the time machine, you will knock on the door. His mother will answer, and you will introduce yourself. It will sound something like this: 'Hello, Mrs. Ellis. My name is Anne, and I am your daughter-in-law. I am from your future, and I've come here with David to have a talk with you.' She will be curious, so don't worry about her shutting the door in your face. Tell her that you married her son and that you have two children. You can give her their names if you so choose. Then, tell her what you have learned about David and his fear of being poor. Choose your words, not mine. Be as creative as you like. Are you ready?"

Anne seemed excited. She looked at David with a different set of eyes. "I am ready."

After a few moments to collect her thoughts, she spoke.

"David, I am going to take you on a special trip, one you have never known in your entire life. It's a trip to your past, and the best part is that we will travel in a time machine. We are in the twenty-first century, and I happen to have one right outside."

Anne looked at David when she offered him the trip. She instantly knew exactly what to say and how to behave. After all, she was the mother of two children, both under eight, and had read several books on parenting. She took on the role as if she had rehearsed it many times.

"Are you ready to come with me?"

Her affect changed to that of a mother talking to a child. Her words were couched in gentle tones, and her language matched.

"Are you sure you want to do this?" said David. "You know my mother. She may not be as open as you hope." They both chuckled. Holding hands, they leaned closer.

"You may be right, but I think I can handle her. Are you ready to go?"

David nodded with a smile.

"Okay, if that's what you want."

Anne made the sounds of a rocket zooming through the air. When she landed, she used the table adjacent to their chairs and knocked three times. Her imagination made the visit seem like a fairytale, and David was sucked right in. *Knock, knock, knock.* Anne acted as if David's mother answered, and she was primed to begin their encounter.

"Hello, Mrs. Ellis. You don't know me, but one day in the future, I am going to marry your son. My name is Anne. It was Anne Housman, but now it's Anne Ellis. I heard a lot about you from your son, and I think it's time you and I had a visit. This is David. He's a grown man now and the father of your two grandchildren. I am sure you are going to meet them one day. Today, I came to share some important information with you. May I come in?"

Anne continued in her role as if she had done this hundreds of times. It always amazed me to see how creative partners can be. I give them little direction, and they take off like a pro.

"David told me it was really difficult growing up with you. He always felt like you were worried about money and that there was never enough. He told me he had the impression that you were going to send him away to live with his grandmother. He developed a great fear of abandonment due to this situation, so money and abandonment have been the core of his wounds until now. I am not sure why you conveyed this message to him, but it had residual effects throughout his childhood and adolescence, and they have remained until now. He always felt threatened and lived in silence with his fears. It has interfered with our marriage because he always feels that I will abandon him due to his perceived inability to provide for me and our kids. Your words, intentional or not, left him with a fear of impoverishment and abandonment, even until today. They have impacted our marriage, and I need you to apologize to him and release him from these fears. You may not have realized the damage you installed, and I'm sure you did not do it on purpose, but you can make amends. It's not too late."

It amazes me to hear the way women can improvise so easily. They embellish the story to give it more power and understanding for their partner. David never had an advocate in his youth to reassure him about his security. Anne was now his champion. Listening to her share his repressed feelings registered an "aha" moment in his mind. It was as though someone understood his pain. It was a relief to hear the words, which had never been in his consciousness, let alone been expressed. He sat silently, listening to Anne until she finished.

"David, is there anyone else you want me to talk to?"

"Yes, my father, but he doesn't live here. He lives in Hawaii."

"No big deal. The time machine is in the front yard. We can zip over to Hawaii in seconds. Let's go!"

David knew his father's address, and when they landed in his front yard, Anne repeated her introduction.

David's father had married his mistress, which was the reason for the divorce. He was quite wealthy and lived a glamorous lifestyle. His two boys, both with his second wife, enjoyed the benefits of a rich daddy! Anne knew that David had been fatherless for most of his childhood, but David had always left out the deep emotions that had triggered, probably because he was mostly not in touch with them. There was always a bravado attached to his story, which is common when we never remove our survival suits.

David had always felt abandoned by his father but tended to idealize him, as he was the absent parent. Although David would visit his father and new family, he felt unwanted, as if he never belonged there, and he was always relieved when it was time to go home. His issues of abandonment, plus his fear of not being able to fix things for his mother, left David feeling unwanted and helpless. This remained deep inside him—until now.

This glimpse into David's life was not uncommon. In fact, the movie *Rocketman*, portraying the life story of Elton John, exemplifies David's life in many ways. Elton John's rocky relationship with his father revealed the abandonment and lack of a secure attachment. He felt that he didn't matter, and as a result, he sought love and approval throughout his life, often in the wrong places. This mirrored David's life in many ways, especially when Elton's father had two more sons with his second wife, giving them what had been denied to Elton. The movie reflected that Elton John had done a lot of therapy with the inner child as part of his recovery.

Back in my office, it was time to visit Hawaii. *Knock, knock, knock*! Once more, the door opened, and Anne pretended that a young male servant answered. She and David had been there many times with their children, so she knew about his father's valet. Anne announced herself and requested to speak to Mr. Ellis. She told David that the valet had answered the door and was inviting them in. Just then, Anne acted like David's father had entered the room.

"Oh, hello, Mr. Ellis. I am Anne, from your future. One day, I will marry your son, David, and become your daughter-in-law. Do you mind if I have a seat? I want to talk to you."

The scene was a repeat except for the dialogue, which was specific to the relationship regarding David and his father. Anne shared her understanding of how David's father's departure—and the fact that he chose to live so far away—had affected David, notwithstanding the impact his new wife and half brothers had on his life.

While Anne spoke with authority and ease about the consequences of this on David, he began to sob, as if he were literally in his father's home. Anne's words had registered deeply with David, and neither he nor Anne had ever experienced this behavior. I placed my hand between them as a reminder to allow the feelings to rise and fall until the wave crested. This took a few moments, all in silence, but when it was over, David looked at Anne with swollen eyes and a sense of peace and satiation. Anne had created a corrective experience for David simply by saying the words he could never share. This was because, up until now, he was not fully aware of how painful the loss of his father had been, and he would have never been able to recite the words that came so easily to Anne. Once again, she was his champion.

Reaching the Other Side

Anne and David crossed the bridge over troubled waters and reached the shore, where they could begin a process of genuine healing. The ritual continued with appreciations and precise words to describe the space between them. David shared his appreciation to Anne and let her know he felt she was a true partner. Anne said that what she appreciated most was David's vulnerability.

Each word described an aspect of their healing. They looked at each other with new eyes and deep, mutual understanding.

"See the new landscape in your partner's face," I said. "Look who's here. It's you, my husband. It's you, my wife."

We took some time to process the experience of Anne as the visitor and David as the host. Before the ritual began, David hoped he could use this to express his discontent and anger with Anne. He imagined that she would be unable to defend her position, as that would have been an illegal import. In his model of reality, it would be a time for him to discharge his anger and resentment without her responding to his monologue. What he learned instead was that content doesn't matter. It's all about the process. There is no blame, only revelation. We need to know what happened to us as children. Intentions do not matter!

After crossing the bridge over troubled waters and reaching the shore to heal, Anne and David were ready to continue with a new sense of hope. This ritual had taken the entire morning to complete. We stopped for lunch and continued until our time was up. David had more he needed to process. He had unfinished business with both parents, which he wanted to address. We spent the afternoon having both his parents, one at a time, do a ritual called "The Child Speaks to the Parent."

During this process, David, using a child's simple language, tells his parents what it was like growing up with them—what hurt him the most and which needs were unmet. With Anne playing the role of each parent, this created an opportunity for David to receive reparations from his parents. Taken together with what had transpired earlier, this became yet another bridge crossing over troubled waters, ultimately allowing Anne and David to arrive safely—and together—on the shores of healing.

What Do We Do Now?

My intention in this book is not to go through every principle and ritual I use in my practice. Instead, I prefer to illustrate the conflicts that arise in most relationships, with the understanding that many of the issues we face are a result of childhood traumas, which often slip through the cracks of our unconscious brain and lodge there until conflict arises later in life.

This is why Hedy Schleifer calls conflict an opportunity and a friend. When a couple learns how to apply this method to their relationship, they will discover that, more than likely, these conflicts arise out of unresolved childhood issues desperately trying to be resolved. The relationship is the platform where we can observe how these issues manifest. They play out in the here and now with the unconscious intention of healing the past, without our knowledge or awareness. That is why Freud called this repetition compulsion and Alice Miller called it the logic of absurdity. We unconsciously hire our mates to help us understand and resolve childhood wounds; then we fire them for doing exactly what we hired them to do.

Therein lies the logic of absurdity. It's my job to call this out and lead my couples across the bridge. Your only job, if you need any help, is to be willing to accept it.

*Like a bridge over troubled water
I will lay me down
Like a bridge over troubled water
I will lay me down.*

—PAUL SIMON

Chapter Eight

Take Charge of Your Fears and Reclaim Your Value

WHY IS IT so difficult to be accountable? Is defending ourselves more important than being honest? Was Socrates right when he said, "A life unexamined is not a life worth living?"

You already know the answers, but let me remind you why you are right.

When we remain defensive, unwilling to come clean about how we feel, we store up layers of shame and guilt, and we may not even be aware of doing so. These feelings may be buried so deep in our subconscious that our default position is to become defensive.

This behavior is prompted by the oldest, most primitive part of our brain—the reptilian "fight-or-flight" mechanism, which keeps asking, "Am I safe?" and "Will I survive?"

As we evolve, we take the elevator up to the neocortex and frontal lobe, which are the most recently developed. They ask reasonable and logical questions and help us work through why we feel the need to defend ourselves. The frontal lobe, which resides in the forehead, processes what the neocortex is thinking.

In other words, it explores our thoughts and allows us to see our behavior as an observer. If we allow ourselves to mature and be introspective, we challenge our own thinking as we work through any negative behavior we may have. This process is essential to achieve healthy, adult relationships.

Defense Mechanisms

We all employ unconscious psychological strategies to protect us from anxiety, which can arise from unacceptable thoughts or feelings when we feel threatened. That's when our defense mechanisms often get in the way. According to Freud, when they become habitual, they can result in neurosis, such as anxiety, phobias, obsessions, or hysteria—for both genders.

You know them, and you use them. In relationships, they are your weapons of protection, but they do not protect you. They can easily become weapons of mass destruction. They are a natural part of the human condition, at least until we learn how to shed our survival suits. Only then can we evolve to a higher consciousness and discover who we really are as our authentic selves. If we maintain our false selves, we cannot learn how to resolve conflict.

In previous chapters, I discussed our survival suits and how we hold on to our false selves to survive—or so we think. Honestly, inhabiting these defense mechanisms ultimately gets us nowhere. What worked in our childhood no longer works when we are trying to create and maintain healthy relationships, not just with our partners but with friends, children, business associates, and colleagues. The only thing that really works is to be in our essence.

Here is a list of defense mechanisms and what they do to protect us.

Denial

This is one of the most common responses we use to defend ourselves. This refusal to accept reality is meant to avoid emotional pain, but it ultimately blocks us from becoming aware of the truth and working our way toward acceptance.

Repression

This occurs when unpleasant thoughts, painful memories, or irrational beliefs are driven into the subconscious corners of our brains.

Projection

We do this when we attribute unwanted thoughts, feelings, and motives to another person. In interpersonal relationships, the easiest way to discharge our unacceptable parts is to project them onto our partner.

Displacement

When we redirect an impulse onto a powerless substitute target, which all too often is our partner, we displace our feelings and shirk responsibility.

Regression

This occurs when we feel threatened or stressed, and our behavior reverts to an earlier stage of development, such as having a temper tantrum.

Rationalization

All too often, we make excuses to justify our behavior.

Sublimation

We do this when we replace unacceptable emotions and behaviors with constructive alternatives that will satisfy the positive intention of our destructive urges. For example, teenagers with aggressive tendencies may channel their aggression into contact sports. Another example might be turning objectionable sexual impulses into music or art. That's when negative energy can be sublimated into positive behavior.

Reaction Formation

This behavior occurs when a person attempts to hide his or her true feelings or desires by demonstrating or adopting the exact opposite feelings. It is used as a defense against anxiety, which can be caused by negative feelings.

Identification with the Aggressor

We see this when hostages establish an emotional bond with their captors, such as during a kidnapping or when a child identifies with an aggressive parent and develops similar behavior.

While this chapter is not meant to be a textbook for Psych 101, recognizing what defense mechanisms you and your partner use can help you understand your behavior and how it affects your relationship.

The Value of Owning Your Dark Side and Making Amends

What is the dark side of a human personality? Carl Jung referred to it as our shadow side. According to Jung, our shadow, instinctive and irrational, is prone to psychological projection when a perceived personal inferiority is recognized as a perceived moral deficiency in someone else. It's that part we don't want to own or realize exists. This part is reprehensible to us, so when we act out this part, we often wonder why and where it came from. Once again, it's as if Jekyll and Hyde live inside us, and we don't know why.

Sometimes, our partner can trigger the worst in us. That

occurs when it fires off earlier feelings of trauma, which may not be in our consciousness. We walk away feeling ashamed and guilty, wondering what made us act in such an unsavory and reprehensible manner. When we recognize the original pain or trauma, we can better understand the cause but not always the cure.

Remember Ellen? When she had a meltdown on her wedding night and broke a vase, her level of frustration had reached overdrive, and she could not contain her anger. There were obvious reasons for her explosion, but if we dig a little deeper, we can understand that she had collected stamps over many years from her family of origin. Her childhood, teenage years, and early adulthood had been filled with volcanic material. When she was unable to receive support from her brand-new husband or her family, she erupted, which was a result of her past frustrations and rage, along with the groom's lack of cooperation. She lost it, which gave her husband a reason to have her Baker-Acted.

If we could rewrite Ellen's life story and learn that she came from a healthy and supportive family, this clusterfuck of a wedding night may have never occurred. Then again, if that were true, she probably wouldn't have chosen Mark as her husband. She was repeating her past with an unconscious desire to fix what had been broken.

I explained this in a previous chapter, but it bears repeating. We unconsciously choose our mates to help us work through childhood wounds. When they do exactly what we "hired" them to do, we fire them! This is why psychologist Alice Miller quotes it as the art of absurdity.

"If we do not work on all three levels—body, feeling, mind—the symptoms of our distress will keep returning, as the body goes on repeating the story stored in its cells until it is finally listened to and understood."

Sound familiar?

Ellen's mood reached a level where she could not contain her anger. Her inner Eliza Doolittle, masquerading as "Hyde," lunged after her symbolic Henry Higgins, when she heaved his slippers with a force so unlike the person she had been trained to become. Ellen reached that level of frustration on her wedding day, which elicited her dark side, and her regression of intense stress triggered a temper tantrum.

In my model of the world, I would say her anger rose from feeling manipulated and controlled by her Svengali (Hello, Mark), who was trying to morph her into someone she didn't want to be. Of course, *My Fair Lady* was fictional, so I have no idea what Eliza's impoverished life might have been about, so I am unable to draw precise dots from her past to a conclusion. But in Ellen's case, we can see the arc of anxiety from her childhood to the altar.

Remember Margie? She became incensed when she discovered one too many times that her boyfriend had a harem he was using for his private entertainment. Since Margie did not have direct access to her neocortex and frontal lobe, her inner Hyde exploded with a vengeance that manifested into physical violence when she pushed him into a closet and beat him relentlessly with her arms and legs. She walked away from that event feeling guilty and ashamed of her primitive behavior and lack of control. When we explored her history, it didn't take long to see that the frustration and anger she had displaced onto her partner was unconsciously intended for her father, who had abused her through his abandonment.

This triggered her fear of poverty and confirmed the insecure attachment she felt since childhood. It was not the same behavior as Brad, her partner, but feelings of betrayal were triggered, and she was beating up both her father and Brad. In Margie's mind, she had been abandoned first by her father, who did not provide financial security, and then by Brad because of his womanizing.

This was a quintessential sadomasochistic relationship. Margie chose Brad to ensure that she would never be impoverished, but the payoff was perhaps worse. She lost herself to create a secure attachment, which she had never experienced as a child.

I worked with Ellen and Margie to investigate their dark side and explore their decision-making process, especially their unconscious choices, which were even more relevant than their conscious choices. That's because the unconscious dictates our behavior.

Ellen had lived with Mark for four years prior to their marriage. Margie had been with Brad for more than five years. Both women's behavior had not revealed itself in a day, a week, or a month. It had been obvious during the entire time these women had been with their partners, with the exception of the courtship period, when everybody put their best foot forward.

While observing the dark side of their partners, each of them continued to maintain the status quo, suffering repeated disappointments. The evidence was revealed over and over, yet they continued to maintain their relationships, thinking they would be able to impact the improvements they were seeking. Despite their partner's predictable behavior, and even when they repeatedly cried their hearts out, leaving the relationship was not an option for either of them. Ellen and Margie were addicted and feared being alone. As they continued to rationalize, their mind games won them over each time they felt disillusionment and heartache.

Ellen and Margie sold themselves a bill of goods. Their insecure attachments and codependency allowed the status quo to remain. When nothing changed, Ellen thought marriage might be the answer. Margie hoped for the same, even though marriage was not a consideration for Brad. He loved the status quo. Margie was the main event in his life, while his harem supplied his drug of choice. Margie remained, come hell or high water, and it was mostly hell. She kept Brad grounded and stable, not unlike the role of a nurturing mother, but it was not fulfilling enough to undo his insatiable need to conquer women. His obsession had a weird and damaging parallel to Margie's insatiable need to conquer him.

Brad used his money and charm to maintain his harem and his relationship with Margie. All the women in his life seemed addicted to his lifestyle and generosity. However, while the harem accepted his wanton desires in exchange for the benefits he provided, that was not the case with Margie. She wanted more—nothing unreasonable, just fidelity and exclusivity, which Brad could not give her or any woman. Margie's attempts to convert him failed miserably, yet she hung in there. Her neurotic needs, a result of her insecure attachment in childhood, continued to fuel her codependency and addiction.

Ironically, Margie was a successful businesswoman. She had her own real estate agency, employing more than a dozen realtors. She earned beyond six figures annually, yet because of her deep emotional wounds, she didn't feel worthy without this man in her life. Her need to conquer Brad was insatiable. Nothing was ever enough. Brad was a player in the top 1 percent of America's wealthy elite, and Margie was willing to sell her soul to the devil to be part of it.

In psychology, we know that you can't fix an internal problem with an external solution. It never works!

As Albert Einstein said, "No problem can be solved from the same level of consciousness that created it."

For Ellen and Margie, the way out of their relationships would come through denying their denial. They had to come clean because their mental and physical health were at risk. After months of intensive therapy, Margie could break the codependency and move on. Ellen had no choice. Mark asked for an annulment, but their marriage ended in divorce. That didn't mean that all was well. It was the beginning of a new and painful journey, and each of them had a lot to learn about themselves, especially how their dark sides had been keeping them from the light.

Childhood wounds run deep, and the consequences of that damage can affect relationships. The lesson is, if you don't embrace your shadow side, it will bite you in the ass!

Healing the Wound and Finding Closure

There are occasions when crossing the bridge to resolve childhood wounds will work for individuals and couples. Although there are multiple spins we can put on the process, the results can often be rewarding. Here is an example of working with a client who needed closure.

For a year, Katie ruminated about seeking professional help. Her best friend, Alicia, convinced her to schedule an appointment. Katie is an attractive forty-six-year-old, a happily married woman with three teenage children: Kim, seventeen; James, fifteen; and Andrew, thirteen. Katie's conflict was not about her marriage or children, although it frequently interfered with both aspects of her life.

Katie had been abandoned by her biological father before her birth because he did not want to be part of her life. He never married Katie's mother and chose not to have anything to do with his child. Although he surfaced occasionally, he never recognized his daughter and denied any responsibility for her. Soon after Katie was born, her mother married, and Katie's stepfather adopted her and became Dad. As soon as she could comprehend the facts of her birth, Katie was told about her biological father. Her parents had two more children, and although they were half brothers, Katie never felt like an outsider. She was treated as if they were all born to the same parents. Even so, her feelings of worthlessness remained lodged in a deep corner of her mind. The rejection and abandonment defined her as not being lovable.

It was difficult for Katie to share these feelings. The

uncertainty surrounding her biological father's abandonment and disinterest in her life left a hole in her soul. Although grateful to her adopted father for raising her with love and support, she did not know why her biological father had chosen estrangement. Katie knew how to contact him, but she avoided it. She defended herself by pretending not to care. She even told me she hated him.

"What kind of man denies his daughter her birthright?" she said. "He's a piece of shit, a dog, and I hate him. He doesn't deserve me. I've managed to become strong and independent without his love and support. Why should I give a shit now? It's his loss. He didn't deserve to have me as his daughter."

Katie began to sob. I waited for the wave of despair to settle. She looked at me for understanding and compassion. I stayed connected with soft eyes. "Why did you seek therapy?'

"I'm not sure. These feelings of rejection have been pervasive throughout my life. They sometimes interfered with my marriage, work, and my relationship with my mother. I couldn't talk to her about this because she wouldn't understand. She would say, 'Why do you even care? You have a dad who loves you and has cared for you since you were a baby.' I ran into the same response with my siblings, my aunt, and even my friends. My biological father's lack of interest and dismissal defined me as not being worthy. It impacted my self-esteem, and I pretended it didn't matter. But it was me who felt I didn't matter."

We sat in silence for a moment.

"I hate him," she said, over and over, with genuine contempt.

I had Katie cross the bridge to express her feelings of abandonment and its impact on her life. She was reluctant to do the process, fearing she would lose her composure. She could mask her feelings with indifference, exchanging her need for love with hate and dismissal, as he had done with her. This was a reaction to her authentic feelings of wanting to be loved and accepted by a father she never knew. Finally, she shared her story of growing up without her biological father, and the feelings of rejection soon caused tears to emerge.

"I don't think I can do this. It's too painful."

I aligned with her fear. "Yes, I am sure it is. Do you want to heal and get closure?"

"I'm not sure. I don't know if it will help. I have lived well all my life without his presence, so why would I want to open wounds I have kept closed all my life?"

Her fear was palpable, which reinforced the repressed pain. "To heal, the wounds you have kept closed must be opened and discharged so you can get closure. Your father is not here, so he can't reject you. What's his name?"

Katie hesitated. Finally, she said, as tears spilled down her cheeks, "S—S—Sam."

"Okay, let's put Sam in the chair."

I set up two chairs facing each other. "Sam will be seated in one and you in the other. Are you with me?"

"I guess so."

"I will teach you how to cross the bridge to meet Sam, your biological father."

"What if I can't do it? What if I don't like what he says? I don't want to learn why he didn't value me as his daughter."

"That won't happen."

I reassured her that it was time to address her feelings, that it would be a key to recovery.

"This takes courage, Katie. This is why you made the appointment to see me, even if a part of you did not want to come. Another part knew what you needed to do, so you made the choice to work through this. Do you want to finally heal this wound?"

Katie nodded and sat in the chair.

"Your father, Sam, is seated in the empty chair before you. He is here now, waiting to hear your voice. Imagine his presence.

Imagine how he looks. This is your chance for change. I will be with you every step of the way."

I reminded Katie that she knew what he looked like because she had seen him at a relative's home. She had seen him many times. Each time, he fell silent in her presence or left. He had always been uncomfortable facing her. Now he would become a willful participant.

"Look at your father and tell him what it was like never having known him."

This time, there was no hesitation. "Oh, my god! It was awful. I couldn't get you out of my mind, always wondering why you didn't care, why you never tried to see me, why you ran away from your responsibilities as a father, why you didn't love me. How could you? I was a baby, not even born yet. Your baby, yet you never showed up. I felt like I didn't exist or matter."

Katie paused as her tears morphed into sobs, mixed with guttural sounds bellowing from her core. I waited for the wave to subside before I began again. "Tell him how he hurt you."

Katie blew her nose and wiped her tears. She took a couple of breaths and sat frozen, unable to speak. I waited silently until she composed herself. "Tell him how he hurt you."

Katie took a few more breaths and wiped her eyes. "You hurt me. You denied my existence. I needed to know you loved me and cared about me, but you never showed up. Damn you! What is wrong with you? What kind of a man are you? You're a loser, a coward, a miserable piece of shit, and I hate you. I hate you! I hate you!"

"Tell him what you needed most from him that he didn't give you. Go ahead, tell him. He's right here in front of you. Tell him." I raised my voice to a pitch she had not heard before.

"I needed you to acknowledge me, to see me, hear me, know I am your child, your daughter, but you never did. You stayed away like a coward, a loser, denying the love I needed and pretending

I didn't. You made me feel invisible, like I didn't matter."

I grabbed a piece of pipe I keep for these moments. Katie revealed her anger as the color of her face changed. I handed her the pipe with instructions to bring it down. It didn't take more than a moment before the pipe slammed hard onto the chair that housed her invisible father.

"Bring it down, Katie. Say, 'I'm angry!'" I gave her permission to express her anger. "Bring it down with force! Let him know how angry you are for abandoning you. Bring it down and say the words, 'I'm angry, I'm angry.'"

The pipe slammed hard against the chair. "You left me. You ran away like a coward, a miserable coward." Katie screamed as she continued to pound the pipe.

"Louder!" She swung the pipe harder and harder, giving her voice the power she had repressed for so long as she denied her feelings. Her anger mounted with each swing.

"I'm angry, I'm angry, I'm angry!" Katie kept shouting until she was physically exhausted. She took several breaths, then tossed the pipe onto the sofa. She looked at me, overwhelmed but seemingly grateful. I waited a few minutes as her breathing returned to normal.

"How do you feel?"

"Tired but relieved. I don't like expressing anger, as it's not how I was raised. I feel lighter and somewhat liberated. Wow! I guess I've been holding on to my anger way too long."

"Yes, you have, and now you gave your child, little Katie, a voice she never knew she had. You are her champion. What you needed from your father that you never got was his love, his acceptance, and his acknowledgment that you are his daughter, his little girl."

There were more tears, but they seemed to be tears of joy instead of sorrow. Katie, the adult and child still within her, smiled at me. "Thank you for setting me free. Anger is not acceptable in my family. Actually, many feelings are not acceptable. Sadness, anger, and fear are never expressed. If I dared to show anger, I was told it was a sin. If I was sad, my father would say, 'I'll give you something to be sad about.' If I was afraid, I was told there was nothing to be afraid of, so I was ashamed if I showed these feelings, and I learned early on not to express them."

"Instead, you became split from what you were told were negative and unacceptable feelings. I guess you buried them, along with your father."

I recited a quote from the Gospel of Thomas, hanging on a chart in my office, which I had memorized.

"If you bring forth what is within you, what you bring forth will save you. If you do not bring forth what is within you, what you do not bring forth will destroy you."

Katie looked at me like an innocent child. There was curiosity and wonder on her face, as if she had had a revelation or epiphany.

"This is a quote from the New Testament," I said.

We both sat in silence as she processed the exercise.

"Close your eyes and see little Katie, the baby who was abandoned by her father."

Katie closed her eyes and followed my instructions.

"Ask her to come forward so you can see her face. You know exactly what she looks like. Notice everything about her—her eyes, how she wears her hair, her clothes. Imagine you can put her on your lap. Hold her right here in your arms."

As I instructed Katie to hold her child in her lap, I placed a teddy bear in her lap, leaned over, and gently placed her arms around the teddy bear.

"Tell her how precious she is—how special—that there has never been anyone like her and there will never be anyone like her again. Tell her she is lovable, smart, and beautiful. You don't need to say these words aloud, only with your heart. She will hear you. Tell her that of all the people she will meet in her life, you are the only one who will never leave her."

Katie cried. She hugged the teddy bear, now a symbol of the child within her. The tears brought her to closure and completion. It was up to her to take care of her little girl, the child who was abandoned and denied love. Katie would have to be the champion this child never had.

What Do We Do Now?

I've worked with many women still suffering as adults from the harm they experienced as children. Each one needed a special form of TLC to break through the logjam of emotions holding them back for so long.

In Katie's case, she hated the man she wanted to love, the man she wanted to love her back without conditions. Her hate was a reaction to the love she had been denied. Her religious training and upbringing had fostered an environment of repressing her feelings until I permitted her to release them. Once that happened, the hurt produced anger. Katie's healing began by honoring the feelings she had not been able to express.

I asked Katie to write a letter to her father, which she didn't have to send. I asked her to write down all the feelings she had harbored silently for so long.

"I wrote the letter. It was hard, but once I began typing, the words came without effort. They just appeared on the screen as if someone else wrote them."

"That's because you released your truth last week. Can you read it to me?"

Katie opened the letter and began. "Dear, Sam . . ."

The poetic letter was written with grief and despair, like a song of woe. As Katie read, her tone changed. Her voice was no longer shadowed by sobs. It resonated with strength as she enunciated each word with conviction. She took deep breaths. A few tears emerged, but Katie stayed with what she had written. Every word came from her limbic system, the seat of emotion in the brain, the part she had cut off to protect herself. Now those feelings were free to surface, and her words became the tool to let her retrieve her inner power.

I listened with gratitude. We had transformed her life into freedom. I felt like a great quarterback, and Katie was a star wide receiver. We created this transformational experience. Her business was not finished. This was only the first chapter.

"Now, if you feel strong, it would be a good idea to meet with Sam and share your letter. It's your call, but I would encourage you to do this."

"What if he won't meet with me? What if he avoids it?"

"Let's cross that bridge one step at a time. Do you know how to reach him?"

"Yes, that's not a problem. I can get his number from my aunt. I just need to think this through. I don't know if I'm ready."

"Take your time. You've waited this long. You must feel ready. I trust you can do this."

Katie nodded. "You are right. This is the last step of my journey."

"I'm glad you see it that way. Even if you never read the letter to him, you have done amazing work. You are a warrior! You have a goddess in you who can take you across the finish line. Her name is Athena. She is an archetypal energy that resides within you."

Katie understood. She felt empowered to do what she had to do.

A week later, she returned, a bit bubbly but still composed. She'd had a very good week and felt resolved and complete. As I listened to her, I noticed her undeniable joy.

"What's going on?"

"I spoke to Sam. I told him I wanted to meet with him. He said he has been waiting for this moment all his life. We met a few days ago."

"Wow! How did you feel?"

"Shocked but excited and even hopeful. I wasn't sure he was going to show up. I expected him to call with an excuse to cancel, but he didn't."

According to Katie, Sam came into Starbucks, their designated meeting spot. When he saw her, he put his arms around her and began to tremble.

"Katie, I waited for this moment all my life, never believing it would happen. How brave of you to reach out to me. I haven't been there for you. I thought this day would never come."

They teared up. Sam owned up to his behavior and how he had abandoned her. He felt more ashamed as the years passed. She spoke his words as if she had memorized them. "'I know I failed you,' he told me. 'Reasons won't matter now. I was stupid, a stupid jerk. I ran away from you, your mother, and all my responsibilities. When I realized what I had done, the shame made me stay away longer. The few times I saw you, I couldn't look in your eyes. I was a bad guy, a lousy father, and too afraid to face you. You were the one who suffered due to my behavior. If you hadn't reached out, I might have never had this moment or the chance to say I'm sorry.'"

Katie continued to detail the conversation. Her words in response to his made me feel that she had attained the closure she had longed for. "I guess you were right," she said.

"That's not important, Katie. You did this! You did what you thought was right. You took care of yourself and little Katie. You made her feel that she mattered. You are, and always will be, her champion."

Katie's closure opened the door to other wounds she wanted to heal. Her success with her father gave her the belief that if she could do that and get the results she hoped for, she had no reason to hide behind her fears any longer. She could do anything. Her newfound empowerment overshadowed the anxiety of opening up other wounds.

Katie reminded me of the beauty of this process. I have always told my clients that when a person decides to commit, the universe cooperates!

The meeting of two personalities is like the contact of two chemical substances: if there is any reaction, both are transformed.

—CARL JUNG

Chapter Nine

Where, Oh, Where Has My Sexy Self Gone?

EVERY RELATIONSHIP HAS its ups and downs. Sometimes, the downs can last longer and do more damage than a partnership can tolerate. Even so, with the proper tools and resources, couples can learn to recognize and communicate their differences, negotiate healthy compromises, and navigate those stormy times, often preventing a breakup because they made a loving and sincere effort to find solutions.

One of the most common problems men and women encounter is sexual dysfunction, which can happen out of the blue at any age. In women, this is usually a symptom of another underlying issue, which may be apparent or lurking somewhere under the surface.

Why Is This Happening?

Sexual dysfunction can occur because of anxiety, depression, stress, poor body image, a history of low self-esteem due to earlier physical and/or sexual abuse, and unresolved anger. These issues can manifest unwittingly and at any time. Sexual dysfunction—and the conflict it brings—can occur because of unresolved issues within a relationship that usually trigger wounds from the past.

Mental and physical illness, as well as attitudes and beliefs formed early in life, are important factors to consider when attempting to identify what contributes to a loss of libido.

Many mitigating circumstances can affect women and men. Alcohol and drugs are major contributors to sexual dysfunction, as are aging, medication, and excessive pornography. Addiction, whether it's alcohol, drugs, or behavior, often fuels disconnection, undermining intimacy. For example, it's not easy to enjoy oral sex while harboring unresolved hostility.

Psychological reasons do not usually arise until a couple has taken their wedding vows or the relationship has progressed to building a family. After the honeymoon stage, the birth of a child can often interfere with the freedom a couple used to enjoy. Once you add more kids, a woman becomes even more exhausted from caring for the onslaught of what her family requires—let alone what her husband needs—so by the time she beds down with him for the night, how can she have any energy left for sex?

Women who work, have kids, and don't have support to lighten their load develop apathy toward having sex due to exhaustion and feeling alone in their effort to keep it all together. Their energy is depleted from a full day at work, followed by children's needs, housework, shopping, dinner, tidying up, and walking the dog. If a partner is supportive and shares responsibilities, there will be energy left for lovemaking. But if a woman takes on these roles and responsibilities alone, sex will fall to the bottom of her to-do list, and her sexual interest will flatline.

Anger will build up, along with a dose of resentment, and sex will be compromised, most often without a conscious thought. In simple terms, under ideal circumstances, family life requires two adults to handle responsibilities, especially when both parents work. If housekeepers are affordable, this can remove some of the burden, if both partners agree to it.

A Shout-Out to Single Mothers

I'm sure you know at least one divorced woman taking care of her kids largely by herself, working, and trying her best to meet her domestic responsibilities. Too often, she doesn't have the time or energy to enjoy a fulfilling sex life, so her sexuality will diminish or disappear.

Time management is the key to (re)igniting her human needs.

Loneliness, when too deep, can be dangerous if it seeps into a woman's life. Her need to connect becomes lost—because of a lack of time and vitality. Even online dating can end in frustration, disappointment, and regret, especially because a bad date is a waste of valuable time!

Of course, this is not always the case. I know many single and divorced women with children who have been successful in finding fulfilling relationships through a plethora of dating services. However, that takes time, patience, a strong constitution, and a good sense of humor. For both genders, rejection runs rampant in the world of online dating. After months and even years of searching for the right mate, giving up is not uncommon.

When the Fairytale Begins

During the initial stages of courtship, sex is vital to cement the relationship and often occupies most of the couple's time. Once we go between the sheets, we fall into a trance, and projections fly everywhere. Magical thinking sweeps us off our feet. It takes us to the moon on gossamer wings as we see and believe what might not even exist. This is nature's way of tricking us into procreating to make more of us while we think our hot sex life is love!

During the honeymoon stage, everybody's singing with their best voices, enjoying the best parts of their romantic sexual aria. This fantasy is portrayed in many films, but life does not always imitate art. Unfortunately, sex drives fade, and reality eventually sets in. What happens then is what matters—after all, that good lovin' has rocked our boats.

"Where is the man who ripped my clothes off, stayed for hours in bed, looked into my eyes, and told me how beautiful I am?"

I often hear this question in my sessions.

Suddenly, out of nowhere, without cause or effect, the person who shared your bed and couldn't get enough of you abruptly loses interest, and the sexuality you once shared becomes yesterday's news. Once the conquest has been accomplished, your sensual, horny Mr. Wonderful becomes disinterested and stingy as he falls asleep, leaving you to your own devices, replacing hours of pillow talk with snoring.

In all fairness, men do not corner the market on this behavior, but still . . .

The Four Stages of a Relationship

Susan Campbell wrote that each stage of a relationship mimics each stage of human psychic development. In the first stage, as infants, we look to our mothers for our dependency needs. This stage is called codependency. It's the stage of "falling in love" when we are adults. All boundaries collapse, and we feel nothing but the magic and splendor of each other's newness. Each partner's needs are met, not unlike how a baby and new mother meet the needs of each other. The baby looks into the mother's eyes. The mother looks down into the baby's eyes, and they share a feeling of being together. That's our first connection, which repeats in the first stage of a romantic relationship when we hear a couple refer to each other as "soulmates."

During the second stage of life, called counter-dependency, a child begins to move away from their mom to explore the world. This is the beginning of what psychologists call individuation and separation, two parts of our normal growth and development.

In relationships, we adjust to the same changes. Boundaries

pop back up, and each partner moves away from each other, noticing the differences rather than the sameness from the first stage. This is when marriages and relationships fall apart, when "soulmate" is dropped and exchanged for labels like dog, asshole, or jerk. It's tough to hang in there and aim for a resolution because things may happen unconsciously, and we are not always able to communicate that. Unresolved childhood issues surface. When our past collides with the present, most of us don't have the conscious awareness, skills, and resources to work it out.

Most people are not aware of how their personal history contaminates their relationships. We grow up in homes with poor role models and use that as our frame of reference for how a relationship should be. We bring in our family systems and unresolved conflicts with our parents and unconsciously want to work it out in our adult relationships. Sadly, we end up repeating patterns from the only modeling we know.

Doing what comes naturally, however, is not necessarily in our best interest.

Without insight and understanding, we tend to fight it out, often unfairly, using blaming, shaming, criticism, contempt, stonewalling, and judgment. Most of this behavior was learned in our own homes. This inevitably causes a rift in the relationship, resulting in sexual disinterest or dysfunction. This is when most couples or individuals come into treatment, and many times, it's already too late to repair the problem.

This is not always the case, however, and I have found that when we can discharge the pain, beliefs, and hurts from the past, everyone has a chance to make a new start. This depends on the willingness of both parties to move forward, if there is enough healthy tissue left to repair. Not every relationship is reparable. Sometimes, irreconcilable differences make it best if couples divorce or break up. Staying together for the sake of the children is not a sufficient reason, as they reap unresolved conflicts inherited from their parents, setting them up to possibly reenact them all over again in their own adult relationships.

According to social psychologist Erik Erikson, the third state of human psychosocial development is called initiative versus guilt.

In relational development, this means declaring independence, which begins in childhood, when we go to school and discover our autonomy and independence. It's our first time away from home, facing issues without Mom and Dad to take care of things. As we learn to do this successfully, we grow more self-assured and build our self-esteem.

In relationships, there is no intimacy without autonomy.

When we reach the third stage in our relationships, not being as needed as in the first and second stages can threaten our partners. Each partner's mental health and maturity will determine how well they work through this stage. It takes two healthy, mature adults to build and maintain a successful relationship, with each party free to enjoy their autonomy. When codependency is the foundation of the relationship, it is doomed to fail unless both partners thrive equally.

In 1492, Rabbi Menachim Mendel of Kotzk, a noted scholar of his time, said, "If I am I, because you are you, and you are you, because I am I, then I am not I, and you are not you. But if I am I because I am I, and you are you because you are you, then I am I and you are you, and we can talk."

This wise man coined the term codependency more than six hundred years ago.

The fourth stage is interdependence. Fifty percent of couples never arrive here because more than half of all divorces take place in the second and third stages. It takes years for this fourth stage to mature, when each partner supports the autonomy of the other and enriches each other's life. This requires relational maturity, self-esteem, insight into owning our own stuff, and becoming enlightened, what some may call *conscious* or *woke*.

It takes two woke people to succeed. Most couples require a therapist to arrive at this stage. The good news? It can be done!

Why Relationships Fail

Throughout these four stages, the most common reaction I see to the anger and hurt that arises in all relationships is getting "turned off." The only exception is when two people agree never to disagree, which does not make for a conscious relationship. Most of the time, sexual dysfunction raises its nasty head because of this turnoff, and it can happen equally to men and women. It is one manifestation of a relationship turned sour that has become polluted over time. If this is the case, each party within the structure of the relational space has personal work to do to resolve issues they may have within their family of origin.

Crossing the bridge is a useful platform to address this.

Most family-of-origin issues are socked away in gunny sacks that eventually transport into the relationship. If these include abuse (physical, emotional, verbal, sexual, intellectual, or spiritual), abandonment, or neglect, then the relationship becomes "a killing field."

Therefore, it is so important that these matters be treated like a broken bone. Without proper treatment and a real reset, they won't heal and will play out in the relational space, polluting and potentially destroying what was once so wonderful.

Most of us enter relationships with unrealistic expectations, and when they are not met by our significant other, we face disappointment, disillusionment, and bitterness. Not surprisingly, our libido diminishes as these expectations are not realized. Changing our expectations is paramount. Poor role-modeling, unrealistic expectations, and childhood trauma are perhaps the most common reasons why relationships fail.

Adding Drugs and Alcohol Into the Mix

There is also another reason. Relationships are prone to failure if one or both parties abuse alcohol and/or drugs. That's because using either one to excess often causes someone to *not* be their authentic self, especially when their addiction contaminates their essence. When this happens, that partner is not fully engaged in their relationship with their mate, and one party ends up having a relationship with an addict, who is dealing with their own survival or false self.

To find relational maturity, both partners must be clean and sober, but this cannot happen if one or both are active in a substance addiction. If only one partner is using, the other can receive support by attending Al-Anon meetings; however, it is unlikely that these meetings can effectuate change in their partner's behavior. Modifying their own behavior does not mean they can manage or police their partner's choices. That decision can only come from the addict.

If both parties are using, they both must decide to become clean and sober. Sobriety, which is essential to a healthy, mature relationship, requires work to achieve a desired outcome. It takes a lifelong commitment to achieve conflict resolution. Once the tools and skills are acquired in treatment, it becomes easier over time to be successful. This can never be achieved if one or both partners continue their addiction.

As a therapist, I cannot support a couple who are active in a substance addiction. They must be in recovery and maintain sobriety for the therapy to be effective.

The Curse of Technology

The onslaught of Viagra, Cialis, Levitra, and other sexually stimulating drugs manufactured for men—with nothing yet that matches them for women—has only widened the gap in the natural process of aging. Men can maintain their sexual prowess with the help of these drugs, while women are left to cope with their natural aging process without chemical support.

This has become a pandemic issue in couples in their fifties and on. While women slow down, men can still behave as if they are in their twenties, thirties, and forties, unless prostate problems arise, which levels the playing field. Sexual aging no longer ensures compatibility.

Our world today, with stressors and variables we cannot control, contributes to a lack of longevity in relationships. Technology has exhausted the human spirit, leaving many in chaos, just trying to keep up. Our minds, and what constitutes our soulful content, cannot expand fast enough to keep up with the pace of innovations. We barely speak to each other. Email and texting have become our new communication. Partners go to bed holding their computers instead of each other. This leaves us little time to nurture each other and keep our happiness in perspective. All in all, this is a setup for disconnection, disillusion, and division.

Perhaps the divisiveness in our country reflects the divisiveness we face in our relationships, not just with our partners but with family, friends, and colleagues. We often add a new dimension to our relationships, wanting to be right instead of happy, and we soon find fault and the worst in each other instead of remembering what brought us together in the first place. We need to slow down, shop less, work together, and heaven help us, turn off our devices.

It is important to work as a team to move forward in restoring our relationships. Maybe we need to reevaluate what is important, become aware of our strengths and weaknesses, and make necessary changes so we can grow old together and build a healthier model of living for our children and grandchildren. Let's hope it's not too late.

The Legend of the Lost Libido or a Primer on Sex Addiction and Sexual Dysfunction

Most people think of sexual dysfunction in men as something related to erectile dysfunction (ED), whether it's premature ejaculation, impotency, or an inability to ejaculate. In women, this takes the form of frigidity, an inability to climax or achieve orgasm, or vaginal pain during stimulation or intercourse.

Hypoactive sexual desire disorder (HSDD), now known as female sexual interest/arousal disorder, is a sexual dysfunction that causes a lowered sex drive in women. Many will pass off the symptoms of HSDD as the inevitable effects of aging or changes in their body.

Both genders can exhibit a loss of libido. Physical issues that can cause low libido in men include low testosterone, prescription medicines, too little or too much exercise, alcohol and drug abuse, and other addictions. There is much more to sexual dysfunction than meets the eye. Although controversial, sexual dysfunction can include sexual addiction.

Barbara's Story

The following story is an example of sexual dysfunction portrayed as a sex addiction, coupled with cross addictions, including drugs, alcohol, an eating disorder, and compulsive shopping.

This is Barbara's cautionary tale:

"I stood alone, not for the first time, with a sense of pride and humility, holding a microphone in my hands once again, about to share my story. I looked around the room and saw the faces of so many brethren trying to pull their lives together, many called 'the old-timers,' some called 'newcomers,' and then those who had relapsed and were trying sobriety for a second, third, or who knows how many times again. I was here in my meeting, what I had come to call my new home, and celebrating my first year of abstinence. My hands were shaking, and I thought my knees were going to buckle. A wave of heat ran through my body. I glanced across the room and focused on the one man who had helped make this day happen. His name was Al, and he had been in AA for thirty-five years, yet we were on the same journey. I knew that if he could do it, I could too. He looked at me as if there was no one else in the room and gave me a smile of confidence. It was like he was saying what I was thinking, so I cleared my throat.

"Oh boy! Where do I begin?" I said. "I've had a great life, one that most women would envy. I had beauty, brains, and a loving husband who was a very successful lawyer. I lived in a gorgeous home on the water, with three beautiful kids and time to do whatever I wanted, with no questions asked, and time to get into so much trouble. However, time, or too much of it, wasn't the culprit. It was my addiction. I was an alcoholic, cross-addicted with cocaine, shopping, and assorted sexual-enhancing drugs, and of course, men. I was an insatiable addict with an eating disorder to boot! I never did anything in a small way. I had a greedy appetite for everything. But my drug of choice was alcohol.

"Although I stopped the use of all other drugs except alcohol, men were still up there in the running. Even while married, I had at least two boyfriends, sometimes at the same time, and each one never knew about the other.

"The fact that I can share my story is a miracle. I should have been dead at least three times, and not from the drugs. My choices were crazy because I was rarely clean and sober. For most of my adult life, in fact, my moods were artificially altered.

"My childhood and teen years were filled with whatever I wanted, whenever I wanted, and wherever I wanted. Most of those things should never have been allowed. However, my parents were addicts, my siblings were addicts, and the only way they knew how to love us was to let us get away with whatever we did. I was coddled, spoiled, and overindulged. I grew up with the idea that I could continue employing this winning formula without too many obstacles, and I learned early on how to bamboozle everyone.

"I didn't know or understand any of this when I married Carl. In fact, I really didn't know much of anything, although I thought I was hot shit. I had a law degree and no idea what to do with it. I was uncertain about my future. I mean, who has any insight at twenty-four?

"Carl and I met in law school. I know that sounds amazing. I had the smarts and the tenacity to see it through. But it felt like an accident that I was even accepted. I was cocky, aggressive, and arrogant, but that was just a cover-up for my insecurities since my addictions had not yet fully blossomed.

"Carl was three years ahead of me. I was just starting when he was finishing. He looked nothing like a lawyer, more like the Marlboro Man, but he never smoked cigarettes. He was a bit rough around the edges, with rugged features, the kind of guy who turned you on or not, nothing halfway. To me, his lack of good looks made him attractive. He was straight as an arrow, tough as nails (on the outside, that is), and sported a new Jaguar instead of a horse. Best of all, he didn't act like a lawyer. He was gentle and kind and had more integrity and humility than anyone I had ever known. Carl came from a very intellectual and severely dysfunctional family. Mine was just dysfunctional. His mom was a writer, and his dad was a physician. My parents were well-heeled, but my dad was in business (often the wrong kind), and my mother never worked outside the home. My dad was a high-functioning alcoholic, and my mother was your classic codependent spouse. I got both—the alcohol addiction and the codependency.

"I guess my saving grace was that even though our family was highly dysfunctional, there was plenty of love to go around. We were enmeshed, according to my therapist, but I always saw it as love.

"At an early age, I took on the role of caretaker/rescuer. I was the youngest of five children, and in many ways, I filled the role of the eldest, even though I had been pampered and spoiled. I coached and nurtured my mother and siblings. Dad had his own agenda and was not interested in my opinion, or anyone else's, when it got right down to it. He had plenty for me though. He told me how to dress, how to wear my makeup, my hair, etc., and some of his compliments felt laced with inappropriate language. I often felt exploited and 'icky.'

"Carl and I were so happy. He joined a large law firm, well-known in our community and nationally. He had a great opportunity to develop his area of interest in tax law. I graduated three years later, and we were married. Our life seemed magical, like a movie. I made him laugh, and he made me feel special. I felt safe with Carl, as though nothing bad could ever happen. When I was in his arms, life was perfect. We spent most of our spare time in bed and soon out on the boat he bought for our first anniversary. I conceived about six weeks after we were married, so there went my career. In all honesty, it was never something I wanted to pursue. I wanted to be married and pregnant and hoped to have lots of kids. When our first child was born, it seemed like life couldn't get any better.

"All that changed as time passed and I grew deeper into my addictions. The nature of addictions is insidious, so I wasn't aware of the hold they had on my body and spirit. It just seemed like part of my lifestyle. Carl also drank and did recreational drugs, but it was different for him. He could go to work and not use, except on weekends. It was not like that with me. I used continuously. I always seemed to have a glass of wine in my hand. I partied with friends, men, and shamefully drank and used drugs during my pregnancies.

"As time passed, I abandoned most of the drugs, except for the alcohol. My eating disorder went unnoticed until Carl caught me purging one morning. He said that he had been suspicious of an eating disorder for a long time because my behavior reminded him of when his sister was bulimic. He recognized the symptoms. After months of arguing and denying, I subjugated my will and went reluctantly into a twenty-eight-day treatment center for eating disorders. Although I learned a lot and attempted to participate in the work, part of me remained the addict who resisted treatment and refused to see her own addictive components.

"I always believed I could stop the behavior whenever I chose. I was in denial. The treatment team tried to address my cross addictions, but like my parents and Carl, I manipulated them into thinking that I had it under control. Not that any of it was a waste of time. I learned a lot, but my other addictions took over my sense and sensibilities, so I managed to convince everyone that I was clean and ready to start my sober life. I had learned this well from my father and brothers, so I was good at selling everyone, myself included, a bill of goods, and I did this way too often.

"I became pregnant with my second child soon after I was discharged from the center and able to stop drinking. The minute I was no longer pregnant, we both went to the bottle—baby and me! Carl noticed but didn't want to see the dangers it posed to our relationship and the kids. He would confront me, but I would have a tantrum or convince him I was not out of control.

"All my behaviors pointed to trouble.

"My drinking kept me in an altered state. Men kept me juggling my lifestyle, and both kept me from being the kind of wife and mother I wanted to be. Today, this is my biggest regret.

"I was not present for our children, yet I continued to have more. By the time our third child was conceived, I was on my way to hell. I managed not to drink heavily during the pregnancy but gulped a sip of wine whenever I could get away with it. Although I knew it was not right, I found ways to rationalize it and manage my addiction. It was like I was living two lives—one with Carl and the kids and one with my lover and family, a.k.a. my addictions.

"Each time I went into treatment, which happened several times, I realized that I was never ready to be treated. I manipulated my way out of anything and everything, controlling everyone around me, until one day I could no longer manage my life. I had no more wiggle room. That was when I hit bottom. They say that until that day happens, you really aren't ready.

"Prior to that, I engaged in multiple affairs and crossed every boundary imaginable. I fucked my friends' husbands, my married fitness instructor, neighbors who showed me attention, and more men than I care to admit. Let's just say I had no will or simply one that ran riot. I don't know if the booze made my appetite for sexual conquests insatiable or if my sexual encounters made me drink more to drown my thoughts and rip out every shred of moral fiber I had.

"I was drowning in my addictions. I lost complete sight of reality—not that I was psychotic, but I couldn't see the harm I was causing, not to my kids, Carl, or myself. I was falling deeper and deeper into a hole that was tearing us apart and destroying our lives.

"At that point, I was spiritually bankrupt. My choices with men were disastrous. They were sociopaths, losers, or mentally unstable. I put myself in harm's way more than once, and each time I was assaulted, I called Carl. He always came to my rescue, even long after we separated. He tried to convince me to get my life together, but all the king's horses and all the king's men couldn't put this Humpty Dumpty back together again.

"Sex with Carl became unbearable. I was insulting, critical, and cruel. I made him feel like less than a man. I told him he didn't know how to satisfy me, that he was a lousy lover, and his cock was too small. The sad thing was that Carl and I were so well-suited for each other. We fit! At least in the beginning, we did. I changed all that. My drinking made me abusive and vitriolic, and I made him responsible for my feelings. Carl didn't stand a chance. He tried so hard to make it right, but no matter how hard he tried, my drinking stood in our way. He didn't deserve my wrath, and I placed him in a 'no win' position.

"Every time I share this, I cry.

"I filed for divorce, probably because I sold myself another bill of goods that Carl and I no longer work as a couple.

"He was devastated, as everything about our family fell apart. I remained stubborn and drunk while Carl was confused and dismayed. He had no choice. I wanted out, but Carl had a trump card that I couldn't beat. He threatened to take the kids away and go for full custody if I continued to drink. The law would support that, and I knew it. That was the day I saw the light. That was the day I chose recovery.

"It has been a long journey, one I will stay in for the rest of my life.

"AA, my therapist, group, sponsor, and some members of the fellowship have pulled me out of my hellhole. I have worked the program one day at a time, and now, when I am celebrating my one-year birthday, I can't believe I have become so clear, conscious, and grateful. I am still working on my moral inventory, making amends, and dealing with all my regrets. The Twelve Steps have guided me through the eye of the needle. The steps have been my salvation. They have healed and liberated my wounded spirit. My fellowship has given me the courage and support I so desperately need, and my therapist has helped heal my wounded child and brought back my authentic self, which has been buried for so long under all my addictions.

"I have my life back, but don't think for one moment that I don't know it can slip away from me if I don't stay diligent and dedicated to my recovery. One day at a time is my mantra.

"The Serenity Prayer is my lifeline to reality.

"I don't have a boyfriend now. I have learned that I need to have a relationship with myself before I can have one with another human being. That's why the program asks you not to get into a relationship for at least a year when you enter recovery. It takes that long to find yourself, and getting involved with someone will prevent or delay that wonder from happening.

"Carl and I are friends now. He is proud of my recovery and growth. We work together as parents in the best interests of our children. They are aware of my recovery. Our lives have become normal and healthy. We treat one another with respect, dignity, and consideration.

"I don't know what the future holds, but I know that whatever it will be, it will be better than anything I have experienced. Every day, I wake up and thank God for making me an alcoholic. If not, I would not be the person I am today."

What Do We Do Now?

Barbara's story, while haunting and horrible, is also uplifting. She demonstrates that no matter how low any of us may go, we always have a chance for redemption. One thing that sticks out for me is how she found a support system and cultivated it in a way that slowly but surely has yielded positive, life-changing results.

Any of you currently struggling with sexual dysfunction and related issues, take heed: if Barbara could turn her life around, so can you! Don't be afraid to seek the help you need, whether it's therapy, a change in diet or exercise, or digging deep to find out what is causing strife in your relationship. Above all, make sure you are being honest with yourself and communicating openly and effectively with the person you care about most.

We are only as sick as our secrets.

—ALCOHOLICS ANONYMOUS

Chapter Ten

Coping with Post-Traumatic Breakup Disorder (PTBD)

I CREATED THE diagnostic term PTBD to call attention to the condition so many women face when their relationship or marriage comes to an end. You won't find this unconventional designation in the traditional DSM 5 because I made it up. It's doubtful to appear in the lexicon of classical psychiatry because even though it can cause PTSD—and even homicide and suicide—PTBD is not considered worthy of a place in the big book of disorders. For now, this affliction is known as PTSD or an adjustment disorder with mixed emotional features, such as depression or anxiety. Honestly, though, no matter what you call it, it means you're fucked!

PTBD can happen from inside-out or outside-in. In the vernacular of psychology, an endogenous depression is usually a result of your genetic or biological constitution, which is most often predisposed from birth. It's the way your brain is wired. Exogenous depression is caused by external stimuli, which results in one form or another of a mood disorder, such as what we see in classical forms of depression or anxiety.

In the case of PTBD, it is caused by something outside yourself—in this case, him––your ex! When a man declares an end to your relationship and you do not have any control over his decision, this will cause sleepless nights, overeating or loss of appetite, panic attacks, diarrhea, and occasionally, infantile rage.

A traumatic breakup causes your neuro-generative functions to go awry. Seeing photos, hearing songs you shared, or passing streets you enjoyed walking together can trigger your visual, auditory, and kinesthetic anchors. These unexpected moments produce tears, shortness of breath, and deep sighs, all signals your heart is breaking. When this behavior leads to hours of conversations with whoever will listen to your heartache, it can make you vomit, like Jill Clayburgh did in the 1978 movie *An Unmarried Woman* when her husband announced, much to her chagrin, he was in love with another woman and wanted a divorce. The awful shock threw Clayburgh's character into a panic, and she became unglued, or as we say off the record, fucked!

What Happens When a Relationship Breaks Up?

No matter how this goes down, it soon becomes a nightmare that feels like it will never end, especially when you didn't see it coming. What actually occurs when your investment of time, energy, and emotions come tumbling down like Jack and Jill, destroying all your hopes, wishes, and dreams? What are the physical and emotional ramifications of this disorder, which can leave you feeling so hopeless and desperate that just taking a shower seems too tough? What goes on inside you when a breakup renders you dysfunctional?

PTBD can elicit grief that triggers a cascade of emotions, which feel interminable and take on a life of their own. Some manifestations of a broken heart can take weeks, months, and even years to overcome, especially if the essence of a relationship was built on an addiction to love—a drug of choice for many women.

The physical and emotional symptoms that accompany

a broken heart can produce palpable pain in your chest and a feeling that part of you is sick and even disappearing. Heartache is real and a common effect of a breakup. You're not crazy! Sleepless nights, erratic weight gains or losses, a devalued sense of identity, and a diminished sense of self-worth are all familiar signs of a broken relationship. If you are experiencing crying spells when you least expect them, sudden outbursts, stomach aches, headaches, diarrhea, murderous rage, frustration, and a feeling that this will never pass—you are having normal reactions to a breakup, especially when it was not your choice.

Losing faith and trust in the opposite sex often accompanies these symptoms. In *Something's Gotta Give*, Diane Keaton plays a prominent playwright who reluctantly abandons her rigid boundaries and falls in love with Jack Nicholson, a recording company mogul with a serious commitment phobia. Once he breaks through her defenses, which she had successfully maintained since her divorce, she loses control and surrenders her love-starved body, mind, and soul to Nicholson, who is unable and unwilling to sustain a monogamous relationship. While trying to discharge her pain and suffering, Keaton's character writes a play about her relationship, crying her eyes out as she pounds her fingers onto the keyboard. Writing her story was her unique way to heal.

Any woman could have had an identical emotional experience at some time in her life. Watching the film unfold, you don't know whether to laugh or cry as you share these feelings of loss and grief. One thing is for certain. The older we get, and the more relationships we have, the better equipped we might become for dealing with the effects of when they don't work out.

Dumpers and Dumpees

Whether you are the one initiating the breakup or on the receiving end of this tragic news, the feelings of the dumper are different from that of the dumpee. Both suffer—but with different emotions and subsequent experiences.

The dumper is usually relieved that the relationship is over, but he or she can experience guilt, self-doubt, and shame. At the same time, the dumpee can be devastated, confused, sad, nauseous, grief-stricken, and lost, usually accompanied by a feeling of malaise. Getting by day to day requires an all-out effort. Feelings of abandonment, loneliness, apathy, self-degradation, and even suicidal ideation are not uncommon.

Women who decide to end a relationship can experience the same emotions as a man. Even when they considered the relationship to be destructive to their well-being and had solid evidence to support their decision, they can feel deep regret and self-doubt about their decision.

Men experience pain and suffering when they are dumped too. The difference is that men traditionally compartmentalize better than women and take a more practical approach to handling rejection. They feel the loss, but they overcompensate by acting out or diving into their work.

In *Something's Gotta Give*, Nicholson immediately continued his conquests with much younger women to avoid commitment and heartache. This may have temporarily masked his grief, but it couldn't erase the loss of being with the only woman he may have ever loved. His heartache morphed into a heart attack caused by stress, which is unacknowledged grief.

You're Not Alone

PTBD is a universal human experience. Today, people marry later, and independent women don't have the same needs as their mothers and grandmothers. Men are more dedicated to finding a successful career than a successful partner, even when their mothers pressure them. This is a generalization, but in my practice, it seems to be the norm.

I have also seen a consistent pattern when it comes to the important distinction between losing a relationship that was based on healthy, adult love and one that was based on some level of codependency. In those cases, the pain lasts longer than six months to a year, which often causes clinical depression, requiring antidepressant or antianxiety medication. When this occurs, it is often a sign of codependency or a love addiction. When a woman feels as if she can't go on without a man, that he, and only he, makes her complete, and her world and happiness depend on him, you can be sure she had a codependent relationship. If her suffering lingers for more than a year, she is showing all the signs of a classic love addict!

If that is the case, someone needs help! Get to a CoDA (codependents anonymous) or Love Addicts Anonymous meeting or find a therapist who specializes in codependency and love addiction.

There is a reason why the struggle to let go is so interminable. It has to do with the history one brings into the relationship, especially when a woman hopes her present relationship will make her past feel better. Stop! That never works. You are the only one who can heal the past to make better choices in the present. PTBD is all too common, and you are not alone.

"Did I Ever Really Matter?"

I hear this question often. You probably mattered in the first stage of your relationship, but his interest waned, and he left you for his own reasons, which he shared or didn't.

The usual answer, if you are lucky enough to receive one, usually goes like this: "It's not about you. It's me. It's just not working for me."

When you want to learn more and understand his shift from "I love you" to "It's not working," you may just get a shrug and "I'm sorry," or he may tell you that he met someone else.

That unexpected dismissal puts a fire in your belly and sends you into shock, with no way to find solace. You feel bewildered, broken, betrayed, and abandoned. In other words, you've been screwed, and there is nothing you can do about it.

You find yourself listening to music with lyrics that define your broken relationship and mental anguish. Harry Nilsson singing "Without You" haunts you morning and night, filling your head with words that could have been written by you. "No, I can't forget tomorrow, When I think of all my sorrow . . . I can't live if living is without you, I can't live, I can't give any more."

You wake up each morning reeling in disbelief, stuck in the nightmare of your relationship being over. Knowing you can't do a thing about it creates a perpetual churning in your stomach, filling every cell of your body, and it never lets you forget you've been fucked. It doesn't matter if you ever mattered, because right now, you just don't—not to him, at least. But here's the moment it can turn. One of my patients' experiences offers us lessons.

Brenda's Brutal Breakup

Brenda called me four times between 9 a.m. and 5 p.m. Her language was muffled with sobs and sighs so deep that I could hear her gasping in between her almost inaudible messages.

"What's going on, Brenda? You left four messages since this morning. You know I don't respond to phone calls until the end of the day."

"It was urgent. I was having a meltdown."

"You know the drill. If you have an emergency, you go to the hospital. That's what my voicemail explicitly says."

"Well, it wasn't a real emergency. I just didn't know what to do. I felt like I couldn't breathe. I vomited and couldn't even keep a sip of water down."

"That's an emergency, Brenda. Why didn't you go to the hospital?"

"It would have been too embarrassing, and I knew you would be the only one who could get me through it. Jacob left. He's gone, never coming back. Says he's had it. Done! Kaput! Oh, my god, I hate him. I hate him!" Her sobbing mixed with her hysterics.

"This is not going to be fixed over the phone, Brenda. You need to come in and address this issue. A surgeon can't do surgery if you are not in the operating room. Your meltdown needs to be treated in a clinical setting and not over the phone."

"Can I come first thing tomorrow morning? I really need your help. I don't know if I can get through the night without your support."

It took a few minutes to calm Brenda down. She had the emotional resources to help herself through this event, but she didn't quite believe it. After reassuring her she would live through this and setting a time that worked for us, she made a noble effort to relax until then.

When Brenda came in the next afternoon, she did not appear relaxed at all. On the contrary, she looked as if she had been through a war zone. She had neglected to shower, put on any makeup, or comb her hair. Brenda was a train wreck. The best visual example I can give is Ellen Burstyn in *Requiem for a Dream* when her hopes and wishes dissolved into the stuff of dreams. Brenda said she hadn't slept all night and had taken more than her prescribed dose of Clozapine, the antianxiety medication prescribed by her psychiatrist.

I had seen Brenda weekly for three months, working on her tumultuous relationship, a classic case of codependency, which is another way to say she had a love addiction.

She and Jacob met online, and there was an immediate collision. When a relationship begins like that, it usually ends in a collision too. Brenda broke every rule in the book by using sex as her weapon of attraction. Jacob reveled in her seduction. During their first six weeks, except for meeting their respective life necessities, Brenda and Jacob spent all their time between the sheets to cement a codependent relationship. Neither was conscious of their intentions, and Brenda was not conscious of creating a dependent relationship with me, her therapist.

For Brenda, talk therapy would be like never flushing the toilet. She needed experiential family-of-origin work. That was not her choice, so she was given another: either capitulate to my direction or find another therapist. I explained that her need to discuss her relationship with Jacob was not helpful to her goal. It only fueled the grieving and served no positive purpose. After three months, she didn't even have an outcome goal. There was nothing on her horizon. I had to lead her into creating a vision so she would know what it would be and how it would feel, let alone how it would impact her life if she reached it.

"Your way isn't working, Brenda, so we must try my way. We need to explore your childhood wounds and talk about what happened to you that would allow yourself to sell your soul to the devil. You have been on a roller coaster with this Don Juan since your time in bed morphed into reality. This is not a movie. It's real life. People don't spend their nights fucking their brains out and thinking it's love, at least not healthy, mature adults."

Brenda looked at me like a lost child. She was a very attractive woman in her midfifties and had been through several Don Juans—different content, same results. They all ended in a breakup decided upon and executed by the man.

She had worked as a paralegal for the same law firm for nearly twenty-five years. She was competent, capable, and resourceful. When it came to relationships, however, she failed miserably. It was as if her brain had a hole in the neocortex related to her cognition. She dove directly into the reptilian portion without considering the consequences. (Remember, alligators eat their own for survival.)

Each man was a legend in her mind and a conquest. Her

stories, albeit different in content, were identical in their structure. They met at a bar. She wore her most seductive attire, and the conquest commenced. She stared him down until she caught his attention. He responded with a flirtatious glance, a wink, and a smile. She puckered her lips and blew him a kiss. Her dragon breath reached clear across the bar, and he inhaled it. That's when the fireworks began. One would think that after a few times playing this game, Brenda learned a lesson—or at least asked herself why she kept repeating the same history.

"Why does this keep happening? Why me? I'm a good person. I'm intelligent, good-looking, and even sexy for my age. These guys can't get enough of me in the beginning, and then it dwindles to a farewell, and they usually blame themselves. I hate that. I fall in love, and then, out of nowhere, I'm unlovable. What did I have that I don't have now? I'm the same woman they met in the beginning. I didn't change. If anything, I got better."

Brenda's whining and lamentations reminded me of Eydie Gormé's musical rendition of "What Did I Have That I Don't Have?" I quickly returned my attention to Brenda, curled up in the corner of my couch with tears rolling down her cheeks.

"The time has come for you to explore the reasons for your behavior. You made these choices. If we look deeply, perhaps we can discover the 'whys' you keep asking about. Brenda, tell me about your childhood. What was it like growing up with your parents?"

"We don't have to go there. What happened in the past is in the past. I had a good childhood. My father and mother worked hard to support us. They never made much money, but they tried hard to please my brother and me. My father drank a bit, but he wasn't an alcoholic. My mother never seemed happy. I don't think I ever saw her smile or heard any laughter, but I know they loved us and did their best, given their circumstances. I really don't want to go there. It brings up some bad memories I don't want to think about. Can't you just tell me what I need to do to stop this crazy merry-go-round?"

"I just did. Wherever you don't want to go is exactly where you *need* to be."

Brenda looked disappointed.

"Look, my parents had their problems, but they did the best they could. I don't want to blame them for my problems. I made poor choices, and now I bear the consequences."

"Yes, you do. You've paid your dues many times, and here you are, at your age, and nothing has changed. Look, this isn't a blame game, Brenda. If we blamed your folks, we would have to go back and blame theirs—and theirs before them. That's not the way this works. Intentions don't matter in this work. You need to know what happened to you."

Brenda's eyes shifted to the ceiling, and she shook.

"What's going on? Let it come up, Brenda! Give it words. Let it come up."

"I can't! I can't! Please don't make me!"

"Yes, you can. You need to get out whatever it is. I'm here with you."

No words came out, just guttural, gut-wrenching sounds mimicking a wounded animal. Brenda pulled her knees closer to her chest and buried her face.

"Brenda! Look at me now. Do you want to get well? Look at me. I'm right here."

After a few deep breaths, she wiped her tears and finally spoke.

"My parents are Holocaust survivors. They were together at Auschwitz and were the only ones left from both their families. Nothing could be worse than what they suffered."

I waited for her sobbing to ease. It only took a few moments but felt like hours. She looked at me like an innocent child, took a few more breaths, and continued.

"I never wanted to go there. My heart hurts just talking about it. My parents are wonderful. They chose to be survivors, not victims. They struggled to care for us and sacrificed everything so we would not feel deprived. They came to America through Israel. My brother and I were born there. I was three when we came here. They worked long hours in a laundry, in the heat, with giant fans that never cooled them down. They came home with damp clothes that had absorbed their sweat.

"My parents both came from large families—seven siblings each, and they were the oldest. Both families perished in those horrible camps. They were the only survivors. They never talked about it. My mother was nineteen, and my father was twenty-three. They were the lucky ones, or maybe they weren't. That's where they met, fell in love, and survived."

I had no words that would suffice, but I stayed present.

"I'm so sorry, Brenda. I didn't know. Three months together, and I never knew. Thank you for sharing. I know how difficult it must be."

Brenda sighed long and hard, and I did too.

"Enough, for now," I said. "There will be plenty of time for more. Let's just rest now. There's always another day."

I felt my tears trying to find a way out. We sat for a few more minutes, and I asked if I could share a meditation. Brenda nodded and allowed her body to relax into the sofa.

We began with breathing.

"Close your eyes, Brenda. Be mindful of your breathing. It's the most fundamental rhythm of life, holding on and letting go. For now, you can hold on to as much as you like, and you can let go as much as you feel safe to do. Just be mindful of your breathing. The air you breathe in and the air you breathe out."

When Brenda returned the following week, she seemed relaxed and volunteered that her mood had shifted since our last meeting.

"I reflected on our session all week and realized I had been holding in what I could not bear to express."

"Yes, I know. You've had this stored with lock and key in the basement of your mind, and it was pleading to be released. Trauma gets locked in the amygdala in the brain."

It was time to teach. I pointed to a large chart identifying the different parts of the brain. I began with the oldest part, the reptilian, and slowly identified each part.

"The reptilian, the oldest and most primitive part of our brain development, asks, 'Am I safe, and will I survive?' It's our fight-or-flight mechanism. It doesn't think about the consequences. It just does whatever it has to do to survive. The limbic system is the seat of our emotions, which asks, 'Is it painful or pleasurable?' Human beings run from pain and toward pleasure. The neocortex is the brain's computer. It asks, 'Is it reasonable and logical?' The reptilian couldn't care less about reason and logic, as it only wants to survive. The limbic goes for pleasure to avoid pain. That's where the trauma is sealed—in the amygdala. It also doesn't care about outcomes or consequences. The neocortex, the limbic system, and the reptilian brain do not interact with one another unless we make that choice. They are independent and exist for their agenda. It's up to the frontal lobe, the newest and most evolved part, to consider consequences and outcomes. It thinks about what the neocortex thinks about. It is the mindful and conscious part of our brain. The intention differs in each part, except the neocortex and the frontal lobe. The others protect you from feeling the pain, not unlike shock absorbers on a car."

I came to my closing mantra, which I have often used with my clients, including one you will recognize from chapter 8. In the Gospel of Thomas, it says, "If you bring forth what is within you, what you bring forth will save you. If you do not bring forth what is within you, what you do not bring forth will destroy you." I read it a few times and asked Brenda to read it with the intention of understanding the meaning as it related to her. Brenda repeated the words. She looked at me with curiosity and wonder.

"I get it," she said. "I get it. This is what I came here for."

I nodded and smiled.

"How do the words resonate with you?"

"I have kept this secret as much as my parents. It always felt like an unspoken covenant. We knew it was there, but we were uncomfortable asking questions. This is why I'm here."

"Yes, this is why you are here and why there was a shift from anxiety and enormous pain to understanding and serenity. You expressed what had been inside you for most of your life, and you have been saved by your self-exploration, which challenged your fears and went unspoken for so long. Maybe having someone here to serve as a benign witness to your suffering and emotional exorcism was significant. You are a courageous woman, Brenda, a real warrior."

She sat quietly for a long time, glancing back and forth at the charts.

"I get it. I get it. I was so unaware of what was behind my compulsion that I sacrificed myself to feel worthwhile and loved."

"Tell me more."

I leaned into her space.

"I think I took on my parent's feelings. Feelings that they didn't matter. Feelings of low self-worth and whatever leftovers they carried out of Auschwitz, which they never shared with my brother and me. I knew about the Holocaust and their time in the concentration camp, but they never talked about it. Whenever we asked, they would say it was not something we should ever know. They were family secrets, but we knew the horrors of their lives. I learned about it in high school with all the books and movies. I tried to carry their feelings so they wouldn't have to carry them. I think my brother did the same. We both have never been able to find happiness and longevity in a relationship. We were carrying our parent's history, along with our own."

"Yes, Brenda, and perhaps now is the time to let it go. Their history is not yours. You have unconsciously inherited your parents' trauma. Do not claim what is not yours. They would not want you to take on their legacy of the Holocaust. It would prolong the suffering to another generation. One was quite enough." I felt Brenda finally let go of much of the weight she had been carrying. Maybe she could finally allow herself to value her own existence.

What Do We Do Now?

What does Brenda's story mean for having a conscious relationship? Being woke in a conscious relationship doesn't just apply to relationships with others, although that is essential. It means connecting with your internal essence, getting in touch with your feelings, and cultivating a conscious relationship with yourself. Ask yourself the following fundamental questions:

Who am I?

What is my purpose?

How do I want to live my life?

Who have I hurt?

What amends do I need to make?

How can I do the right thing?

These are the same questions Jews ask themselves on Rosh Hashanah, the Jewish New Year, and curious people worldwide, no matter what their religion or culture might be, also ask one way or another. Even as things change, these philosophical questions are foundational components in the world of psychology and within cultures throughout the world.

If we can develop higher consciousness and mindfulness, especially in our relationships, our lives will be enriched. If we can address each other with appreciative inquiry and respect, our relationships will thrive.

"Am I willing to commit to a fulfilling and meaningful life and a healthy and happy relationship?"

This is a question each of us must ask, and if you answer yes, then keep reading!

*Out beyond ideas of
wrongdoing and rightdoing,
there is a field.
I'll meet you there.
When the soul lies down in that grass,
the world is too full to talk about.*

—JALAL AL-DIN RUMI

Chapter Eleven

A Conscious Relationship

AFTER RETURNING HOME from an ECCT master class reunion in Italy in May 2018, I received a letter from a woman named Judith, a colleague who helped coordinate the event and was reaching out to all of us who attended.

Two months later, Judith passed away after a courageous struggle with pancreatic cancer. She left a legacy of the lessons she learned during her fight, which complemented what she practiced during her life's work. Her missive, a portion of which is included here, highlights the most salient questions she asked herself before she passed, even when she did not know her days were numbered.

A Love Letter

Hi, dearest friends,

Saying goodbye has been difficult and coming back to Paris even more difficult. I guess you could say I am experiencing 'separation anxiety.' I miss you all. Today, I felt lost, sad, tired, not wanting to eat, and have been listening to music and hanging out in bed.

I have been reflecting on what is going on, pondering this question all day. What has suddenly emerged is my experience during our gathering of love and secure attachment. Many of us did not know 'secure attachment' as children. I, for one, did not, and I have been working on this throughout my cancer journey with 'cellular memory' as an amazing tool.

I started thinking about these questions: What is love, and what does it feel like to be 'securely attached'? I am referring to love and secure attachment on an 'essence or soul level' rather than an 'ego level.'

Here are the words I came up with: feeling loved for who I am, not what I do, feeling safe, feeling secure that someone will protect me, feeling seen and heard, feeling able to be vulnerable, feeling loving eyes, feeling loving touch, feeling cherished, adored, unique, special, and appreciated for my differences and talents, feeling accepted when my behavior is different from others.

The experience of this allows me to feel securely attached. The three days we spent together demonstrated all that for me. Each day, our connection deepened until there was a space of love and trust where I felt secure and safe and able to share with you deeply and honestly and to receive you with respect, love, and curiosity.

Thank you, each and every one of you, for being who you are.

It was more than a three-day gathering of ECCT therapists for me. It was an experience of being with loving, accepting, highly conscious people who make space to receive the other, fully and unconditionally. This experience will live on in me, and my life will be different because of it.

I bow to each of you. I love you.
Judith

What Is a Conscious Relationship?

Judith was my beloved friend, a kindred spirit, a wizard therapist whose memory will live on within every soul she touched and every life she transformed. This book is dedicated to her.

Her responses are the best description I can offer to a question many of us should ask: "What is a conscious relationship?" The answer doesn't emerge out of the blue. It is not acquired in a moment, a year, or even (for many) a lifetime. For individuals and couples, it takes a genuine commitment to create and maintain conscious relationships. We are not born knowing how to do that; developing the necessary skills, tools, resources, and mindfulness takes practice and desire. While some may have parents who modeled a conscious relationship, it does not occur as often as we would like because every family is somewhat dysfunctional.

The term "conscious relationship" didn't exist in most of our families of origin. Virginia Satir, the founder of family therapy and a great therapist in her own right, was considered a pioneer in marriage and family therapy. She treated her first family in 1951, when it was considered highly unconventional.

We've come a long way since then. It is only in the last thirty years that we have discovered the invaluable insights that therapists like Satir promoted. We finally understand the importance of creating and maintaining conscious, mature, and healthy relationships.

Judith's whole career was dedicated to asking the right questions and recognizing the appropriate answers. It was as if her understanding arrived just in time—two months before her demise, when she shared her insights with us. Her generosity of spirit is an example of someone who kept searching for answers to questions that most of us never ask.

The tragedy of tragedies is to face your death and not know who you are. Judith searched deeply, inspired by Gerard Manley Hopkins, an English poet and Jesuit priest in the 1800s, who left us all a provocative quote. "What I am is me for that I came." She also echoed the words of Lao Tzu. "When I let go of what I am, I become what I might be."

Judith's quest reminds me of Herman Hesse's *Siddhartha*,

whose spiritual journey was one of self-discovery. In her own way, Judith exemplified and embraced the most important questions and answers we must learn and integrate on our own path to conscious relationships. She and her beloved husband modeled the essence of this type of ultimate union.

A Litmus Test

How do you relate to the feelings Judith described in her missive?

Are you loved for who you are and not what you do?
Do you feel safe?
Do you feel secure that someone will protect you?
Do you feel seen or heard?
Can you be vulnerable in your relationship?
Do you feel loving eyes, a loving touch upon you?
Do you feel cherished, adored, unique, and special?
Do you feel appreciated for your differences and talents?
Do you feel accepted when your behavior is different from others?

If you answered "yes" to these questions, then we can say you are living and feeling securely attached in a conscious relationship.

If you answered "no" too many times, it's time to learn how to achieve these essential feelings and share them with your partner. After all, you cannot give what you do not have.

Love and Lessons from Oz

Love is difficult to define because it is subjective and means different things to different people. In *The Road Less Traveled*, M. Scott Peck, MD, wrote one of the most brilliant definitions of love I have ever read: "Love is the willingness to extend one's self in order to nurture another person's spiritual growth."

Are you doing this in your relationship? Be brutally honest and accurate when answering the above questions. It's easy to justify, defend, deny, project, blame, and sell yourself a bill of goods. If you want to grow, look inside. Practice mindfulness and consciousness.

Most people can't do this alone. They need a benign witness, a therapist trained to help navigate the process. It is not the Wizard in *The Wizard of Oz* who leads Dorothy and her friends down the yellow brick road. She must wind through the dark green forest to find her way back home. The Lion represents the courage she is seeking. The Scarecrow symbolizes her mind, and the Tin Man, her heart. It is only when Toto, Dorothy's dog and security blanket, leaps out of her arms that her vulnerability transforms into empowerment. She is left alone to delegate and fight her way to freedom. When she does, she arrives at a place of true self-love.

The dark green forest filled with lions and tigers is there to motivate us, not deter us from finding ourselves. Only after Dorothy kills the Wicked Witch of the West does her higher power appear in the form of Glenda, the Witch of the East. She comes down from the clouds and tells Dorothy to click her heels so she can return home to Kansas. Dorothy, distressed and weary from her search, yells back at Glenda, "Well, why didn't you tell me that in the first place?"

"If I had, you wouldn't have believed me. You had to go through the dark green forest to find your way home."

This is exactly what needs to happen if we want to know ourselves. Not unlike Dorothy or Judith, who sought the truth, it takes time, patience, and commitment to follow the yellow brick road and discover who we are.

I am not sure if L. Frank Baum, the author of *The Wizard of Oz*, had any idea of the impact and meaning his story would have on self-discovery, but we can all be thankful he inspired the great artists of Hollywood to create his splendid tale.

It's easier today to travel down the yellow brick road than it was for Dorothy and even Siddhartha. We have more practical ways to make the journey to self-discovery. Group therapy, a process I facilitated for decades, is perhaps the most successful modality I know to learn about your essence. If taken into consideration with positive intention, the feedback received from others can be very helpful, even to the most resistant and skeptical patient.

That's because there is always a window that does not allow us to see what others find so easy to see in us. When the same issues keep rising, you know these are patterns begging to be addressed. When a handful of fellow citizens give you the same feedback, only a fool would not consider listening and looking inside. The answers are there. It takes a conscious mind to allow the unconscious to emerge.

What Is Mindfulness?

According to Mission Be, an organization devoted to promoting social learning and stress reduction in schools, "Mindfulness can be described as the practice of paying attention in the present moment and doing it intentionally and with non-judgment. Mindfulness meditation practices refer to the deliberate acts of regulating attention through the observation of thoughts, emotions and body states."

In today's whirling world of technology, hectic schedules, and perennial responsibilities, it is difficult to stay present. It is an art to learn, not unlike presencing. That is why we see so many classes and programs teaching mindfulness. Our world is spinning so fast that if we do not live in the moment, it is easy to forget what really matters.

We must take stock of what is truly important and what is not. What is important to a thirty-year-old is not as important when you are fifty or sixty years old. When you reach my age (eighty-five), it's all relative. Ask a twenty-five-year-old what's important. You might get an answer about finding a soulmate, reaching career goals, staying fit and thin, having a nose job, a boob job, a bubble butt, and so on. As we age, our interests and goals change. Staying healthy is vital. For a millennial, who may be taking life for granted, staying healthy is not as big as finding their passion, a boyfriend or girlfriend, spending three days at a music festival, or passing the MCATs. Our culture has changed, though, and young people are more aware than their parents ever were about the benefits of living a healthy lifestyle. They are also into mindfulness in ways that previous generations were not.

A Lonely Road

Growing old is not easy without a partner. If you are divorced, never married, or widowed, it gets tougher. That's compounded if you are over sixty, because after living life alone, compromise can be difficult. You get used to not having to make your bed, going to sleep when it's convenient, skipping a shower, eating eggs with ketchup, watching your favorite TV shows, and not having to deal with toilet seats that never get put down.

However, this solitary life can also be lonely and depressing.

Are dating sites the answer? Creating a profile online can be risky, like walking through a minefield. Do you advocate for gun control? Conservative or liberal? Any answer can trigger a deluge of negative responses. You might find the perfect guy, but after a few dates, developing feelings for him, you learn that he is a recruiter for the NRA, which goes against your values.

These issues never used to come up. You could have political preferences and differences, which may not be aligned, but now, almost any contrast can become a dealbreaker. What's a girl to do? Be true to yourself. Be mindful before acting on a whim or through magical thinking. Remember what Freud said, which Deepak Chopra added to when he said, "There are no accidents! There is only some purpose that we haven't yet understood."

Differences will arise and cause conflict. Easy to enter, difficult to escape.

Relearning the Golden Rule

What does this have to do with a conscious relationship? Everything! Consciousness and mindfulness are essential for having a quality relationship with yourself and your partner. The quote, "Physician, heal thyself," applies to knowing yourself, to attend to your own faults, as opposed to pointing out the faults of others. Until you have a positive relationship with yourself, you will not be able to have a successful relationship with someone else.

It's never too late. In ECCT, couples counseling includes learning about yourself and your partner. It's not essential to go to individual counseling. Exploring your shortcomings, inhibitions, fears, and maladaptive behaviors can be accomplished in the context of couple's therapy. ECCT provides the principles and rituals that create outcomes you might have never thought possible. It is truly what Schleifer espouses—"an adventure in intimacy."

This process is no different from the personal introspection Jews are asked to conduct on the High Holidays or addicts do as the fourth and fifth step of a twelve-step program. It's all about delving deep into our souls, taking a moral inventory of our past, and making amends to those we have hurt while active in our addictions.

A moral inventory does not only include regrets and shameful behavior. It allows us to recognize the best of ourselves. The content may differ, but the structure of purging our souls from behavior that has hurt others is equal to the redemption we can find in making amends. To move forward, we must complete the past.

In *Flatliners*, medical students want to know what happens

when we die. Each student takes turns to see what they experience. As they are moved to the brink of death, they are brought back to life by the others, only to hear the same story repeated about making amends to those they hurt during their lifetime. None of them could go forth without doing so. We know this to be true in the concept of karma. In Hinduism and Buddhism, the sum of a person's actions in this and any previous state of existence is viewed as deciding their fate in a future existence. In real time, you must own your shadow side, reviewing your past that caused pain and suffering to others, and make amends. Apologizing to victims of your bad behavior must be owned as you ask for forgiveness.

The Bible supports the idea that you reap what you sow. In Job 4:8, it says that those who seek trouble usually find it. In Matthew 26:52, it indicates that those who are violent could come to a violent end. Luke 6:37-38 says, "Judge not, and you will not be judged; condemn not, and you will not be condemned; forgive, and you will be forgiven." These passages offer directions to live, with different resources pointing the way forward with the same intentionality.

On the first or second evening of a Tony Robbins workshop, he asks his participants to identify those who hurt them most and have caused unresolved anger and resentment. As a homework assignment, he requests that people go to their rooms and call perpetrators from their past who still have power over them because they are holding on to these negative feelings. He asks that they forgive them for their wrongdoings. This is not done for the benefit of the perpetrator. It is to free up energy, which is keeping those wounded souls stuck in the muck and mire of negative feelings, which are still there long after the original abuse.

This is an exercise in letting go. Anger and resentment are known as e-motions—energy in motion. While embodied in our minds and hearts, we absorb useless energy, which can be sublimated in productive and meaningful ways. By forgiving, you are liberating yourself and clearing the space for positive energy to enter. Forgiveness and making amends morph into happiness. Ponder that! Hard to believe we learned this basic stuff in kindergarten. "Do unto others as you would have others do unto you!"

How quickly we forget.

What Do We Do Now?

It's time to step into the glorious abyss. Who have you hurt? Who has hurt you? What must you do to clean the slate? What questions remain unanswered? What do you need to do to assure that you can have a conscious relationship?

The answers are clear. Look deep and hard because if you are genuine and sincere in your search, the answers lie within you. Why not reach out to those who can support your journey? Going into the unknown is always scary, but it's a vital part of the human experience. No one escapes. It's how we handle it. Do we have faith? Can we trust ourselves?

Nike says, "Just do it!" The subliminal message here might be that if you can't do it alone, seek professional help. When Victor Frankl was asked how he coped with his experience in the concentration camps, he said faith and purpose was his answer, not hope. Hope comes and goes. Faith is forever. Purpose gives you the will to live.

"What was really needed was a fundamental change in our attitude toward life," Frankl said. "We had to learn ourselves and, furthermore, we had to teach the despairing men, that it did not really matter what we expected from life, but rather what life expected from us. We needed to stop asking about the meaning of life, and instead think of ourselves as those who were being questioned by life—daily and hourly."

We hear words of wisdom all the time. Many leave our conscious awareness moments after we read them. Sometimes, these pearls appear as platitudes or clichés because they are expressed so often, which can dilute their profound meaning. However, if you allow these messages to register, they can be valuable. Just sift through Facebook and Instagram, and you will see them daily, making screensavers and soundscapes across our screens. I have many of them framed and on the walls of my office. Sadly, I doubt that many take the time to read them.

Consider one by Abraham Lincoln. "And in the end, it's not the years in your life that count. It's the life in your years."

Although words matter, they alone cannot effect change. Words do not have the power to transform our behavior or beliefs. Change comes from digging deep into the places we want most to avoid. It needs more than words of wisdom. If words were the answer, then all we would need to do is listen to the messages of Joel Osteen, Wayne Dyer, Martin Luther King, Jr., Jesus, Moses, and all the prophets and sages who have graced this Earth.

But there is no magic fix for an internal problem with an external resolution. Whatever you do, don't keep doing the same thing over and over, expecting a different result. Einstein said, "You can never solve a problem on the level on which it was created."

Do you really want to argue with Einstein? If you want an easy fix, watch Bob Newhart's STOP IT! on YouTube. If nothing else, you will get a good laugh. Meanwhile, take a chance on yourself because, after all, you're all you've got, and that's plenty good enough!

Acknowledgments

THIS BOOK REPRESENTS the culmination of all the knowledge I have acquired over my career as a psychotherapist. It would be selfish of me not to share this with you, with the hope that you will benefit from my life's work. But this would not have been accomplished without the support of many people, and I want to acknowledge those who have made this possible.

First, I want to express my gratitude to all my clients, who have defined so much of my professional life. Sharing in the time and effort it has taken to achieve their goals has been enormously rewarding.

My deepest appreciation to Nancy Rosenfeld, my literary agent, who always believed in this book and encouraged me to have it published.

I want to extend my gratitude to my editor, David Tabatsky, whose talent took a diamond in the rough and polished and cut it into a gem, and to Hedy Schleifer, whose wisdom and teachings lent substance and knowledge to its content.

My sincere appreciation to John Koehler and Joe Coccaro of Koehler Books, who thought it worthy of being published, Miranda Dillon, for her copy editing, and Suzanne Bradshaw, for her design work.

I feel honored and blessed that you, my readers, have bought this book and helped make it known to others. You are all part of the fabric that will hopefully make this a bestseller!

Last, I want to thank my children, Monica, Todd, Erika, Aaron, my life partner, Paul, and my fur baby, Minnie . . . for their patience and understanding.

Love,

Joan

References

Bradshaw, John. 2005 (Revised). Health Communications, Inc.

Gray, John. 1993. *Men Are from Mars, Women Are from Venus*

Henrix, Harville, Ph.D. and Helen LaKelly Hunt, Ph.D. 2019 (Third Edition). *Getting the Love You Want*. St. Martin's Griffin.

Lipton, Bruce, Ph.D. 2016. *The Biology of Belief*. Hay House.

Miller, Alice. 1997. *The Drama of the Gifted Child*. Basic Books.

Peck, M. Scott, MD. 2003. *The Road Less Traveled*. Touchstone.

Perel, Esther. 2007. *Mating in Captivity: Unlocking Erotic Intelligence* Harper Perennial.

About the Author

JOAN E. CHILDS, LCSW, has been in clinical private practice as a psychotherapist since 1978. As a clinical social worker, Joan specializes in encounter-centered couples therapy. She is also an expert in codependency, inner-child work, original pain work, and second stage recovery.

She was the first affiliate of the John Bradshaw Center in the United States. She is a certified master practitioner for neuro-linguistic programming, a certified EMDR, a master practitioner, a certified grief counselor, a certified hypnotherapist, a certified life coach, and a PAIRS LEADER (practical application for intimate relationship skills). She has appeared on many national television shows, including *The Oprah Winfrey Show*.

Joan is the author of *The Myth of the Maiden: On Being a Woman* (HCI Books 1995) and *Why Did She Jump? My Daughter's Battle With Bipolar Disorder* (HCI Books 2014). She had her own television series, *SOLUTIONS*, dedicated to the memory of her daughter, Pamela Anne Glassman, which provided information and resources for the community, especially for patients and families with loved ones suffering from mental and mood disorders. She is the founder of the Pamela Anne Glassman Educational Center, in cooperation with the Mental

Health Association of Southeast Florida.

Joan has published many articles on women's issues, relationships, grief, and loss, which have appeared in several well-known online publications, including *The Huffington Post*. She also has an active presence online with her monthly blogs, which can be found on her website, www.joanechilds.com, and she can be seen here: https://www.youtube.com/user/joanechilds.